IS APOSTLE JOHN
STILL
ALIVE TODAY?

By: Philip Mitanidis

IS APOSTLE JOHN
STILL
ALIVE TODAY

By: Philip Mitanidis

BEEHIVE PUBLISHING HOUSE INC.
www.beehivepublishinghouse.com
E-mail: info@beehivepublishinghouse.com

Is Apostle John Still Alive Today?
First Edition 2015. Printed in USA.
ISBN 978-0-9866246-7-4

Published works by the author:
The Creator of Genesis 1:1—Who is He?
The Covenant—A contract Rejected
No God and Saviour Beside Me
According to a Promise
Christians Headed into the Time of Trouble
Ghosts Demons and Dead Men
Moses Wrote about Me
What is the Sign of Thy Coming and the End of the World
The Sign in Matthew 24
Is Apostle John Still Alive Today?

Dedicated to:
"the two witnesses"

All Scripture is quoted from the Old King James Version (OKJV) of the Bible, unless otherwise stated.

I have placed in brackets words or a word to clarify the meaning of the preceding word in some references, which I have quoted from the Old King James Version (OKJV) Bible. I also have translated the Hebrew word "יהוה" and the Greek word "Κυριος" to read "LORD" whenever the Scriptures refer to God the Creator of Genesis 1:1. Furthermore, I capitalized the first letter of the pronouns, which refer to God the Creator of Genesis 1:1.

Please refer to the Hebrew and to the Greek inspired Scriptures in order to verify my opinions.

Greek Scriptures are taken from: Η Αγια Γραφη, Βιβλικη Εταιρεια, Αθηναι, 1961.

Front and back covers and artwork in this book are produced by the Author (Philip Mitanidis).

FOREWORD

If you believe the claims of the book of Revelation, you would believe in the "spirit of prophecy" because the "Spirit of prophecy" is "the testimony of Jesus Christ." And likewise "the testimony of Jesus Christ is the Spirit of prophecy."

Apostle John writes:

> "10 And I fell at his feet to worship him. And he said unto me, See thou [you] do it not: I am thy [your] fellowservant, and of thy [your] brethren that have the testimony of Jesus: worship God: for the testimony of Jesus is the spirit of prophecy." Revelation 19:10

As you have read above, "the testimony of Jesus" Christ the LORD are the words, which Apostle John "bare record" in the book of Revelation. Therefore the words in the book of Revelation "is the spirit of prophecy."

Consequently, if you know the words of "the testimony of Jesus," and God the Holy Spirit reveals to you the meaning of these words, then you will have an understanding of "the testimony of Jesus," which "is the spirit of prophecy."

But, by knowing the words of "the testimony of Jesus" and understanding the meaning of the words of "the testimony of Jesus," does not make you a prophet or a prophetess, as some claim. All it does, like the angels of Christ the LORD, you can claim, "I am thy [your] fellowservant, and of thy [your] brethren that have the testimony of Jesus: worship God: for the testimony of Jesus is the spirit of prophecy" (Revelation 19:10).

And because you are simply given understanding of the words of "the testimony of Jesus," and you are able to reveal the meaning to others, in doing so, let me say again, it does not make you a prophet.

Furthermore, the prophet of the LORD writes about "the testimony of Jesus Christ," and plainly states that it is,

> "1 The Revelation of Jesus Christ, which God gave unto Him, to shew unto His servants things which must shortly come to pass; and He sent and signified it by His angel unto His servant John:

> "2 Who bare record of the word of God, and of the testimony of Jesus Christ, and of all things that he saw." Revelation 1:1, 2

Accordingly, since Apostle John "bare record of the word of God, and of the testimony of Jesus Christ," we should believe what Apostle John wrote in the book of Revelation. But, if we choose not to believe his "record" of "the testimony of Jesus," which is in the book of Revelation, why should we believe the other four books Apostle John has written?

And, if we go down that road, why should we believe Jesus Christ's "testimony"? And even worse, why should we believe God the Father because he was the one who gave it to Jesus in the first place?

Consequently, we have to make a choice. We can accept what God the Father gave to Jesus Christ, and accept what Jesus Christ gave to His angel, and what the angel of Christ the LORD gave to Apostle John, and what Apostle John has given to us, via the book of Revelation. Or, we can reject God the Father, God the Christ, the angel of Christ the LORD, and at the same time, reject Apostle John's "testimony of Jesus"?

But, if we accept "the testimony of Jesus Christ," we are given a blessing right from the start when we begin to read "the testimony of Jesus Christ," which Apostle John "bare record" 2,000 years ago.

Here is the reference:

"3 Blessed is he that readeth, and they that hear
the words of this prophecy, and keep those
things which are written therein: for the time is
at hand." Revelation 1:3

Although it is unfortunate to hear so many times from
the zealot clergy, politicians, and students of the Bible that the
book of Revelation is hard to understand, it is figurative,
symbolic, sealed, etc., let me refresh your memory; when a
person reads "the testimony of Jesus Christ" ("the spirit of
prophecy") that person receives a blessing right away. And, as
far as not being able to understand the book of Revelation,
Apostle John writes:

"10 And he saith unto me, Seal not the sayings
of the prophecy of this book: for the time is at
hand." Revelation 22:10

Since "the time is at hand," and the "prophecy" is not
"sealed" in the book of Revelation, logically and Scripturally,
"the prophecy" in the book of Revelation is being revealed
today to God's penitent people, wherever they are on planet
earth, in order for them to make public, and warn of the
humongous devastating coming events of the "prophecy," to a
perishing world.

The prophecy starts by addressing all of the churches in
the world, which accept the Bible as the word of God, and
form their religious doctrine (Jews, Muslims, and Christians).
These churches are all identified by the name of Laodiceans.
And the Laodiceans are given a stern warning because of their
apathetic attitude toward the word of God and toward Jesus
Christ the LORD. The Laodiceans are said to be "neither hot
or cold" and unrepentant. In fact, they brag that they are rich
and therefore need of nothing.

The stern warning by Jesus Christ the LORD of hosts

to the Laodiceans is as follows:

"14 And unto the angel of the church of the Laodiceans write; These things saith the Amen [Christ], the faithful and true witness, the beginning of the creation of God [Christ];

"15 I know thy [your] works, that thou [you] art neither cold nor hot: I would thou [you] wert cold or hot. 16 So then because thou [you] art lukewarm, and neither cold nor hot, I will spue thee [you] out of My mouth.

"17 Because thou [you] sayest, I am rich, and increased with goods, and have need of nothing; and knowest not that thou [you] art wretched, and miserable, and poor, and blind, and naked:

"18 I counsel thee to buy of Me gold tried in the fire, that thou [you] mayest be rich; and white raiment, that thou [you] mayest be clothed, and that the shame of thy nakedness do not appear; and anoint thine eyes with eyesalve, that thou mayest see. 19 As many as I love, I rebuke and chasten: be zealous therefore, and repent. 20 Behold, I stand at the door, and knock: if any man hear My voice, and open the door, I will come in to him, and will sup with him, and he with Me. 21 To him that overcometh will I grant to sit with Me in My throne, even as I also overcame, and am set down with my Father in his throne. 22 He that hath an ear, let him hear what the Spirit saith unto the churches." Revelation 3:14 - 22

Therefore, the last church, Laodiceans, which consist of all of the churches, which believe and use the Bible to form their religious doctrine has stagnated. It has fragmented. It has not grown spiritually. It has failed to fortify itself with all of the "doctrine of Christ" (2 John 9). Instead. It has survived by adding words to the "prophecy," by deleting words from the "prophecy," or rejecting the "prophecy" of the book of Revelation; and therefore it falls under severe condemnation

> "18 For I testify unto every man that heareth the words of the prophecy of this book, If any man shall add unto these things, God shall add unto him the plagues that are written in this book:

> "19 And if any man shall take away from the words of the book of this prophecy, God shall take away his part out of the book of life, and out of the holy city, and from the things which are written in this book." Revelation 22:18, 19

Therefore, when the angel of Christ the LORD said to Apostle John "Thou [you] must prophesy again" (Revelation 10:11), and the clergy, politicians, Imams, Rabbis, theologians, priests, and laymen, reject the angel's literal command of the words of "the prophecy," it's like rejecting the angel's command. And by rejecting the angel's command to Apostle John, people are in essence deleting the angel's words of the command. And by deleting the angel's literal command to Apostle John ("Thou [you] must prophesy again"), a person condemns herself or himself because we are told,

> "19 And if any man shall take away from the words of the book of this prophecy, God shall take away his part out of the book of life, and out of the holy city, and from the things which

are written in this book." Revelation 22:19

Very strong language don't you think?

So, why would anybody add words or delete words and tamper with the book of Revelation? In fact, why tamper with any of the books of the Bible when there is just as severe condemnation for not believing the words of the prophets of old that are in the Bible (2 Thessalonians 2:12), and for adding words or deleting words from any of the verses of the Bible?

Apostle Paul warns:

> "9 As we said before, so say I now again, If any
> man preach any other gospel unto you than that
> ye have received, let him be accursed."
> Galatians 1:8

Therefore, when Scripture says that Apostle John is going to live "till" they see Christ coming "in His kingdom," should we not believe Scripture?

And when Jesus Christ the LORD of hosts says that Apostle John shall not taste death until such time Jesus comes "in His kingdom," should we not believe the words of Jesus Christ the LORD?

And, if we choose not to believe the words of Christ the LORD, do we then also choose not to believe the words of God the Father?

Remember, the words of "the testimony" were first given by God the Father to Jesus Christ the LORD. And from Jesus Christ to His angel, and the angel was the one who gave "the testimony of Jesus Christ" to Apostle John. And it was Apostle John who "bare record" of the "testimony of Jesus" Christ in a book, which reveals Apostle John will remain alive on earth until Jesus comes "in His kingdom."

Therefore, would you disbelieve Apostle John or the angel of Christ the LORD that Apostle John is still alive on earth today? Or are you going to disbelieve Jesus Christ the LORD and God the Father that Apostle John is still alive today, and getting ready to appear in Jerusalem for three and a half years to "prophesy again" before kindred, tongue, and nations before Satan kills him, and leaves his dead bodies in one of the streets of Jerusalem to rot?

Whether you want believe or disbelieve, the 2,000 year old "prophecy" that Apostle John is still alive today, and lives on earth, as it is presented to us in the book of Revelation, it's your choice to make; all I can do is to simply point you to the "prophecy." The rest is between you and Jesus Christ the LORD of hosts.

The author

CONTENTS

v.   Acknowledgement and Abbreviations

vi.   Foreword

xiii. Contents

14.   The Apostles and Their Fate.

60.   The Book of Revelation an Overview
     68). The Testimony of Jesus
     72). A Warning
     74). A Messenger Sent to Apostle John
     95). "You must prophesy again"
     98). Revelation 10 (OKJV)

99.   The Two Witnesses
     99). The Measurements of the Temple
     103). The Altar of Incense
     105). Measuring the Worshippers
     112). The Court

115.   Empowering the Two Witnesses to "prophesy"
     129). Duration of "prophecy"
     129). Clothed in Sackcloth
     132. Who Stands Before the God of the Earth?
     133). Who is the God of the Earth?

135.   What Prophets are Still Alive Today

141.   Who are the "two witnesses" of Revelation
     chapter eleven?

152.   The Last Call to Repentance

173   A Possible Scenario

192   Revelation 11 (OKJV)

194   Supplements
     194). Revelation Chapters 8 & 9 (OKJV)
     197). Comparative info on the "two witnesses"

199   Questions

THE APOSTLES & THEIR FATE

The question of what was or is the outcome of the twelve disciples, who were ordained by Jesus as apostles, and what happened to the seventy disciples who followed Jesus and performed all manner of miracles in His name, has become a sort of a battle of wits between the historians and the traditionalists?

But irrespective of the on going tug of war between the historians and the traditionalists, the Scriptures of the Bible have a different point of view. And that view began early in Christ's ministry when Jesus had two of John the Baptist's disciples following Him. The gathering and fellowship with the disciples was almost instantaneous. In fact, it began right after Christ's baptism, which took place in the Jordan River.

According to Apostle Luke, when Jesus was about thirty years old (Luke 3:23), He began His missionary work from His hometown of Nazareth, which is located in the province of Galilee on the most southern west side of Lake Galilee. From there, Jesus made it a point to go and see John the Baptist who was baptizing repentant sinner for the remission of their sins. At one point when John the Baptist was talking to the crowed and baptizing the people in the Jordan River, near the Dead Sea, John the Baptist saw Jesus coming unto him; and when He did, John the Baptist said,

"29 Behold the Lamb of God, which taketh away the sin of the world.

"30 This is He of whom I said, After me cometh a man which is preferred before me: for He was before me. 31 And I knew Him not: but that He should be made manifest to Israel, therefore am I come baptizing with water.

The Apostles & Their Fate

"32 And John bare record, saying, I saw the
Spirit descending from heaven like a dove, and
it abode upon Him.

"33 And I knew Him not: but he that sent me to baptize
with water, the same said unto me, Upon whom thou [you]
shalt see the Spirit descending, and remaining on Him, the
same is He which baptizeth with the Holy Ghost.

"34 And I saw, and bare record that this is the
Son of God.

"35 Again the next day after John stood, and two of his
disciples;

"36 And looking upon Jesus as He walked, he
saith, Behold the Lamb of God!

"37 And the two disciples heard him speak, and they
followed Jesus. 38 Then Jesus turned, and saw them following,
and saith unto them, What seek ye? They said unto Him, Rabbi,
(which is to say, being interpreted, Master,) where dwellest thou
[You]?
"39 He saith unto them, Come and see. They came and
saw where He dwelt, and abode with Him that day: for it was
about the tenth hour.
"40 One of the two which heard John speak, and
followed him, was Andrew, Simon Peter's brother. 41 He first
findeth his own brother Simon, and saith unto him,

"We have found the Messias, which is, being
interpreted, the Christ.

"42 And he brought him to Jesus. And when Jesus

The Apostles & Their Fate

beheld him, he said, Thou [you] art Simon the son of Jona: thou [you] shalt be called Cephas, which is by interpretation, A stone.

"43 The day following Jesus would go forth into Galilee, and findeth Philip, and saith unto him, Follow me. 44 Now Philip was of Bethsaida, the city of Andrew and Peter.

> "45 Philip findeth Nathanael, and saith unto him, We have found Him, of whom Moses in the law, and the prophets, did write, Jesus of Nazareth, the son of Joseph.

"46 And Nathanael said unto him, Can there any good thing come out of Nazareth? Philip saith unto him, Come and see.

"47 Jesus saw Nathanael coming to Him, and saith of him, Behold an Israelite indeed, in whom is no guile!

"48 Nathanael saith unto Him, Whence knowest thou [You] me? Jesus answered and said unto him, Before that Philip called thee [you], when thou [you] wast under the fig tree, I saw thee [you].

> "49 Nathanael answered and saith unto Him, Rabbi, thou [You] art the Son of God; thou [You] art the King of Israel.

"50 Jesus answered and said unto him, Because I said unto thee [you], I saw thee [you] under the fig tree, believest thou? thou [you] shalt see greater things than these.

"51 And He saith unto him, Verily, verily, I say unto you, Hereafter ye [all of you] shall see heaven open, and the angels of God ascending and descending upon the Son of man." John 1:29-51

The above disciples were the early disciples picked by

The Apostles & Their Fate

Jesus Christ the LORD of hosts, which was at the beginning of His three and a half years of Ministry to the House of Judah (Jews). But, Jesus did not stop with these handful of disciples. Jesus had other seventy disciples, who testified for Him. He chose twelve disciples in total to ordain during His three and a half years of missionary outreach; but one of them called Judas Iscariot was brought in the group to be a disciple of Christ by the disciples. And at the end, as you probably already know, he turned against Christ and betrayed Him to evil hands. Nonetheless, Jesus was willing to give Judas Iscariot a chance to repent. Therefore Jesus treated him as part of the group.

And as a group, Jesus went "13 up into a mountain, and calleth unto him whom He would: and they came unto Him. 14 And He ordained twelve, that they should be with Him, and that He might send them forth to preach, 15 And to have power to heal sicknesses, and to cast out devils:

> "16 And Simon He surnamed Peter;
> "17 And James the son of Zebedee, and John the brother of James; and He surnamed them "Boanerges, which is, The sons of thunder:
> "18 And Andrew, and Philip, and Bartholomew, and Matthew, and Thomas, and James the son of Alphaeus, and Thaddaeus, and Simon the Canaanite,
> "19 And Judas Iscariot, which also betrayed Him:

On top of these twelve apostles, Jesus had over seventy other apostles (Luke 10:1, 17; 6:13) who followed Him while He was alive, and were sent to do missionary work in His name throughout the region. Unfortunately, at one point, many of the disciples "walked no more with Him." They left Christ; and when they did, Jesus said to the twelve, "will ye also go away?" (John 6:66, 67). Little is known about the seventy disciples after Jesus Christ's crucifixion and resurrection took place.

The Apostles & Their Fate

But, in regards to the eleven apostles who went everywhere with Jesus before His death, the disciples testified that Jesus did appear to them after His resurrection in order to instruct and expound some of the Scriptures they still did not understand.

Apostle Luke, the physician, testifies little bit different from the other Gospel writers, in regards to the events, which took place after Christ's resurrection, but clearly highlights Christ's interaction with the apostles as follows:

"1 Now upon the first day [Sunday] of the week, very early in the morning, they came unto the sepulchre, bringing the spices which they had prepared, and certain others with them. 2 And they found the stone rolled away from the sepulchre. 3 And they entered in, and found not the body of the LORD Jesus. 4 And it came to pass, as they were much perplexed thereabout, behold, two men [angels] stood by them in shining garments: 5 And as they were afraid, and bowed down their faces to the earth, they said unto them,

"Why seek ye the living among the dead?

"6 He is not here, but is risen: remember how He spake unto you when He was yet in Galilee,

"7 Saying, The Son of man must be delivered into the hands of sinful men, and be crucified, and the third day rise again.

"8 And they remembered His words,

"9 And returned from the sepulchre, and told all these things unto the eleven, and to all the rest.

"10 It was Mary Magdalene, and Joanna, and Mary the mother of James, and other women that were with them, which

The Apostles & Their Fate

told these things unto the apostles. 11 And their words seemed to them as idle tales, and they believed them not.

"12 Then arose Peter, and ran unto the sepulcher [Apostle John also ran with Peter to the grave]; and stooping down, he [Peter] beheld the linen clothes laid by themselves, and departed, wondering in himself at that which was come to pass.

"13 And, behold, two of them went that same day to a village called Emmaus, which was from Jerusalem about threescore furlongs. 14 And they talked together of all these things which had happened. 15 And it came to pass, that, while they communed together and reasoned, Jesus himself drew near, and went with them. 16 But their eyes were holden that they should not know Him.

"17 And He said unto them, What manner of communications are these that ye [all of you] have one to another, as ye walk, and are sad?

"18 And the one of them, whose name was Cleopas, answering said unto Him, Art thou [You] only a stranger in Jerusalem, and hast not known the things which are come to pass there in these days?

"19 And He said unto them, What things? And they said unto Him, Concerning Jesus of Nazareth, which was a prophet mighty in deed and word before God and all the people: 20 And how the chief priests and our rulers delivered Him to be condemned to death, and have crucified Him.

"21 But we trusted that it had been He which should have redeemed Israel:

"and beside all this, to day is the third day since these things were done.

"22 Yea, and certain women also of our company made us astonished, which were early at the sepulchre; 23 And when

The Apostles & Their Fate

they found not His body, they came, saying, that they had also seen a vision of angels, which said that He was alive. 24 And certain of them which were with us went to the sepulchre, and found it even so as the women had said: but Him they saw not.

"25 Then He said unto them, O fools, and slow of heart to believe all that the prophets have spoken: 26 Ought not Christ to have suffered these things, and to enter into His glory?

> "27 And beginning at Moses and all the prophets, He expounded unto them in all the scriptures the things concerning himself.

"28 And they drew nigh unto the village, whither they went: and He made as though He would have gone further. 29 But they constrained Him, saying, Abide with us: for it is toward evening, and the day is far spent. And He went in to tarry with them.

"30 And it came to pass, as He sat at meat with them, He took bread, and blessed it, and brake, and gave to them. 31 And their eyes were opened, and they knew Him; and He vanished out of their sight.

"32 And they said one to another, Did not our heart burn within us, while He talked with us by the way, and while He opened to us the scriptures?

"33 And they rose up the same hour, and returned to Jerusalem, and found the eleven gathered together, and them that were with them,

> "34 Saying, The LORD is risen indeed, and hath appeared to Simon.

"35 And they told what things were done in the way, and how He was known of them in breaking of bread. 36 And

The Apostles & Their Fate

as they thus spake, Jesus himself stood in the midst of them, and saith unto them, Peace be unto you.

"37 But they were terrified and affrighted, and supposed that they had seen a spirit.

"38 And He said unto them, Why are ye troubled? and why do thoughts arise in your hearts? 39 Behold My hands and My feet, that it is I myself: handle Me, and see; for a spirit hath not flesh and bones, as ye see Me have. 40 And when He had thus spoken, He shewed them His hands and His feet.

"41 And while they yet believed not for joy, and wondered, He said unto them, Have ye here any meat [food]?

"42 And they gave Him a piece of a broiled fish, and of an honeycomb. 43 And He took it, and did eat before them. 44 And He said unto them,

> "These are the words which I spake unto you, while I was yet with you, that all things must be fulfilled, which were written in the law of Moses, and in the prophets, and in the psalms, concerning Me.

> "45 Then opened He their understanding, that they might understand the scriptures,

"46 And said unto them, Thus it is written, and thus it behoved Christ to suffer, and to rise from the dead the third day: 47 And that repentance and remission of sins should be preached in His name among all nations, beginning at Jerusalem. 48 And ye are witnesses of these things.

> "49 And, behold, I send the promise of my Father upon you: but tarry ye in the city of Jerusalem, until ye be endued with power from on high.

The Apostles & Their Fate

"50. And He led them out as far as to Bethany, and He lifted up His hands, and blessed them.

"51 And it came to pass, while He blessed them, He was parted from them, and carried up into heaven.

"52 And they worshipped Him, and returned to Jerusalem with great joy:

"53 And were continually in the temple, praising and blessing God. Amen." Luke 24:1-53

After the apostles witnessed Jesus going to heaven (Acts 1:11), they all assembled in the upper room in Jerusalem day after day in prayer;

"1 And when the day of Pentecost was fully come, they were all with one accord in one place. 2 And suddenly there came a sound from heaven as of a rushing mighty wind, and it filled all the house where they were sitting. 3 And there appeared unto them cloven tongues like as of fire, and it sat upon each of them. 4 And they were all filled with the Holy Ghost, and began to speak with other tongues, as the Spirit gave them utterance." Acts 2:1-4

After that, they began to preach the Gospel of Jesus Christ the LORD (Mark 1:1) with power and authority in the name of Jesus to the House of Judah (Jews) in their synagogues, on the streets, in their villages, in their towns, in their cities, and in their homes. Their efforts brought converts to Christ the LORD by the thousands. And that success brought the unreserved wrath of the Jewish Sanhedrin upon the apostles and upon the converts who converted to Christianity.

Stephen, one of the seven deacons, after the Apostolic Church was organized, was stoned to death for his evangelical efforts to convert the Jews to Christ the LORD God of Abraham. The leader of the band of people who stoned

The Apostles & Their Fate

Stephen was Saul (Paul) who later repented on the road to Damascus; and after three years of study and meditation in Arabia (Galatians 1:17-19), he became an untiring missionary-evangelist for Christ the LORD of hosts.

But meanwhile, the floodgates of hate for the messenger and for the message of the Gospel of Jesus Christ did not subside after Apostle Paul's conversion to Christianity. They were unleashed by the Jews upon the apostles, and upon those who preached Christ, just as they were unleashed upon Jesus Christ our LORD.

Nonetheless, after Saul, whose name was changed to Paul, was accepted by the apostles who were in Jerusalem; he and Barnabas, a converted Jew from Cyprus, embarked on their First Missionary Journey (45-47 AD). During their travels, they went on the Sabbath days (on Saturdays) to Antioch, Iconium, Derbe, and Lystra to preach to the Jews in their Synagogues. And likewise, when they came from Perga and entered Antioch in Pisidia, they went into one of the Synagogues and sat down; and after the reading ended,

> "15 of the law and the prophets the rulers of the synagogue sent unto them, saying, Ye [all of you] men and brethren, if ye [all of you] have any word of exhortation for the people, say on."
> Acts 13:15

Then Apostle Paul stood up and said, "26 Men and brethren, children of the stock of Abraham, and whosoever among you feareth God, to you is the word of this salvation sent. 27 For they that dwell at Jerusalem, and their rulers, because they knew Him [Christ] not, nor yet the voices of the prophets which are read every sabbath day, they have fulfilled them in condemning Him. 28 And though they found no cause of death in Him, yet desired they Pilate that He should be slain.

The Apostles & Their Fate

"29 And when they had fulfilled all that was written of Him, they took Him down from the tree [cross], and laid Him in a sepulchre.

"30 But God raised Him from the dead:

"31 And He was seen many days of them which came up with Him from Galilee to Jerusalem, who are His witnesses unto the people. 32 And we declare unto you glad tidings, how that the promise which was made unto the fathers, 33 God hath fulfilled the same unto us their children, in that he hath raised up Jesus again; as it is also written in the second psalm, Thou art my Son, this day have I begotten thee.

"34 And as concerning that he raised Him up from the dead, now no more to return to corruption, he said on this wise, I will give you the sure mercies of David. 35 Wherefore he saith also in another psalm, Thou shalt not suffer thine [your] Holy One to see corruption. 36 For David, after he had served his own generation by the will of God, fell on sleep [died], and was laid unto his fathers, and saw corruption: 37 But He, whom God raised again, saw no corruption.

"38 Be it known unto you therefore, men and brethren, that through this Man is preached unto you the forgiveness of sins:

"39 And by Him all that believe are justified from all things, from which ye [all of you] could not be justified by the law of Moses.

"40 Beware therefore, lest that come upon you, which is spoken of in the prophets;

"41 Behold, ye [all of you] despisers, and wonder, and perish: for I work a work in your

The Apostles & Their Fate

days, a work which ye [all of you] shall in no
wise believe, though a man declare it unto you.

"42 And when the Jews were gone out of the synagogue,
the Gentiles besought that these words might be preached to
them the next sabbath [Saturday].

"43 Now when the congregation was broken up, many
of the Jews and religious proselytes followed Paul and
Barnabas: who, speaking to them, persuaded them to continue
in the grace of God. 44 And the next Sabbath [Saturday] day
came almost the whole city together to hear the word of God.

"45 But when the Jews saw the multitudes, they were
filled with envy, and spake against those things which were
spoken by Paul, contradicting and blaspheming.

"46 Then Paul and Barnabas waxed bold, and
said, It was necessary that the word of God
should first have been spoken to you: but seeing
ye [all of you] put it from you, and judge
yourselves unworthy of everlasting life, lo, we
turn to the Gentiles." Acts 13:26-46

After Paul and Barnabas returned from their First
Missionary Journey to Antioch, they went to Jerusalem, about
49 AD (Acts 15:36-41), to attend the Jerusalem Counsel of the
apostles; and while in Jerusalem, they planed their Second
Missionary Journey, which Barnabas included the assistance of
John Mark. But, since Apostle John Mark did not want to go
with them past Pamphylia, on their First Missionary Journey,
Apostle Paul considered John Mark to be unreliable; therefore
he did not want him to go with them on their Second
Missionary Journey.

This disagreement caused Paul and Barnabas to go their
separate ways. Barnabas and John Mark went to Cyprus. And

The Apostles & Their Fate

Apostle Paul took Silas and traveled through Syria to Cilicia and Galatia to visit many of the churches that were set up during his first Journey there. And from there they were going to go to the provinces of Asia and Bithynia, but God the Holy Spirit forbade them. Instead they were instructed to go to Macedonia. And on their way from Macedonia, they traveled through Greece, preaching the Gospel of Jesus Christ the LORD of hosts to the Corinthians. And from Corinth they took a boat to Ephesus. And from there they went to Caesarea in Palestine, and from there to Antioch in Syria.

Apostle Paul, about 53 AD, returned one more time to Galatia on his Third Missionary Journey.

And after their Third Missionary Journey, Paul and Silas eventually returned to Jerusalem to see the brethren. And while they were there, Apostle Paul and a handful of men went to the Temple in Jerusalem and preached the Gospel of Jesus Christ to the Jews. And when the Jewish authorities heard him speak they prepared to take him and prosecute him. But, the Roman soldiers intervened and Apostle Paul found himself carted away under the soldier's protection.

Although Apostle Paul was temporary under the soldier's protection, he found himself spending time in prison for the next two years in Jerusalem and in Caesarea. He first appeared before Felix and Festus, the Roman procurators; and later Apostle Paul was interviewed by Herod Agrippa 2nd and Bernice. The interviews appeared in Paul's logic unfavorable; therefore he chose to appear before the Roman senate instead of the Jewish Sanhedrin. At his request as a Roman citizen, he was transferred to Rome. Eventually Apostle Paul's case came up and he appeared before the senate to defend his case; Paul was tried after two years and was acquitted. And, as a free man, Apostle Paul continued with his missionary work in the name of Jesus Christ the LORD.

After he was exonerated, some historians suggest that

The Apostles & Their Fate

Apostle Paul went west from Rome into other countries baptizing converts to Christ. But, his mission work was not concentrated in Europe; he went to Crete, Nicopolis, Ephesus, and to the city of Troas in Mysia. And, according to legend, Apostle Paul was arrested again and taken to Rome to be prosecuted. It is said that he was confined in the Mamertine dungeon, which is located near the Roman Forum and was put to death as a martyr sometime in the vicinity of 66-68 AD.

Although Apostle Paul states,

"6 the time of my departure is at hand.

"7 I have fought a good fight, I have finished my course, I have kept the faith:

"8 Henceforth there is laid up for me a crown of righteousness, which the LORD, the righteous judge, shall give me at that day: and not to me only, but unto all them also that love His appearing" (2 Timothy 4:6-8),

Like most of the other apostles, Scripturally, Paul's actual day and year of his death eludes us with the exception of the death of Judas Iscariot, who betrayed our LORD Jesus Christ, and James the son of Zebedee, who is better known as the brother of John.

Nonetheless, here are the results of the twelve apostles.

Judas Iscariot who betrayed Jesus Christ our Savior with a kiss to the priests and elders of the people was the son of Simon, a native of Judea, and therefore the only one of the twelve disciples who was not from the province of Galilee. Judas Iscariot was the treasurer (John 13:29) and an opportunist. Way before the LORD'S Supper took place in the upper room, Judas Iscariot already had struck a deal with the priests and elders of the people to betray and deliver Jesus in their evil unrepentant hands. But, knowing what Judas had already done covertly and unknown to the eleven disciples, Jesus said to them,

> "2 Ye [all of you] know that after two days is the feast of the passover, and the Son [Christ] of man is betrayed to be crucified.

> "3 Then assembled together the chief priests, and the scribes, and the elders of the people, unto the palace of the high priest, who was called Caiaphas, 4 And consulted that they might take Jesus by subtilty, and kill Him. 5 But they said, Not on the feast day, lest there be an uproar among the people."
"14 Then one of the twelve, called Judas Iscariot, went unto the chief priests, 15 And said unto them, What will ye give me, and I will deliver Him unto you? And they covenanted with him for thirty pieces of silver. 16 And from that time he sought opportunity to betray Him." John 26:2-5; 14-16
.   And while Jesus was yet speaking to His four sleepy disciples, in the Garden of Gethsemane, "47 behold a multitude, and he that was called Judas, one of the twelve, went before them, and drew near unto Jesus to kiss Him.

> "48 But Jesus said unto him, Judas, betrayest thou [you] the Son of man with a kiss?

> "49 When they which were about Him saw what would follow, they said unto Him, LORD, shall we smite with the sword? 50 And one of them smote the servant of the high priest, and cut off his right ear.
"51 And Jesus answered and said, Suffer ye [all of you] thus far. And He touched his ear, and healed him.

The Apostles & Their Fate

"52 Then Jesus said unto the chief priests, and captains of the temple, and the elders, which were come to Him, Be ye [all of you] come out, as against a thief, with swords and staves? 53 When I was daily with you in the temple, ye [all of you] stretched forth no hands against Me:

"but this is your hour, and the power of darkness.

"54 Then took they Him, and led Him, and brought Him into the high priest's house." Luke 22:47-54

"53 and with him were assembled all the chief priests and the elders and the scribes." "60 And the high priest stood up in the midst, and asked Jesus, saying, Answerest thou [You] nothing? what is it which these witness against thee [You]?

"61 But He held His peace, and answered nothing. Again the high priest asked Him, and said unto Him, **Art [are] thou [You] the Christ, the Son of the Blessed?**

"62 And Jesus said, **I am:** and ye [all of you] shall see the Son of man sitting on the right hand of power, and coming in the clouds of heaven.

"63 Then the high priest rent his clothes, and saith, What need we any further witnesses? 64 Ye [all of you] have heard the blasphemy: what think ye? And they all condemned Him to be guilty of death.

They blind folded Christ, "65 And some began to spit on Him, and to cover His face, and to buffet Him, and to say unto Him, Prophesy: and the servants did strike Him with the palms

The Apostles & Their Fate

of their hands." Mark 14:53, 60-65

"1 When the morning was come, all the chief priests and elders of the people took counsel against Jesus to put Him to death: 2 And when they had bound Him, they led Him away, and delivered Him to Pontius Pilate the governor.

Meanwhile, "3 Judas, which had betrayed Him, when he saw that He was condemned, repented himself, and brought again the thirty pieces of silver to the chief priests and elders, 4 Saying, I have sinned in that I have betrayed the innocent blood. And they said, What is that to us? see thou [you] to that.

> "5 And he cast down the pieces of silver in the temple, and departed, and went and hanged himself.

"6 And the chief priests took the silver pieces, and said, It is not lawful for to put them into the treasury, because it is the price of blood. 7 And they took counsel, and bought with them the potter's field, to bury strangers in. 8 Wherefore that field was called, The field of blood, unto this day.

"9 Then was fulfilled that which was spoken by Jeremy the prophet, saying, And they took the thirty pieces of silver, the price of Him that was valued, whom they of the children of Israel did value; 10 And gave them for the potter's field, as the Lord appointed me." Matthew 27:1-10

Judas Iscariot betrayed Christ the Savior of the world and Creator of "all things" in the hands of evil men for thirty pieces of silver, which would be equivalent on today's market approximately sixteen US dollars an ounce.

What was he thinking?

Obviously Judas was thinking that man could not render the death penalty upon Christ the LORD to take place; and therefore it was OK to make some extra money. But, after

The Apostles & Their Fate

he heard the verdict and Jesus did not defend Himself, Judas was horrified of Christ's outcome. Therefore, Judas repented during his anxiety, anger, and mental duress before sinful un-repented priests and elders of the House of Judah, instead of repenting before Jesus Christ the LORD. And when he reached a saturation point, he chose to do himself harm by hanging himself from a tree. Judas died in 31 AD a cruel and gruesome unnecessary death by his own hand and by the hungry animals, which ripped his limbs and guts out of him and ate them.

Sin has no mercy upon the un-repented sinner (Romans 6:23).

James the son of Zebedee, was the brother of the beloved Apostle John, who was one of the four apostles of the inner circle of Christ, which consisted of Andrew, Peter, James, and his brother John.

Shortly after the crucifixion and resurrection of our LORD Jesus Christ, Claudius, emperor of the Roman Empire, in 41 AD, made Herod Agrippa (I) ruler over Judea and Samaria also, giving him equal authority over the provinces his grandfather Herod the Great had up until 6 AD. Notably, from 6 AD up until 41 AD, the provinces of Judea and Samaria were ruled by the procurators that were set up by the Roman authority.

And when Herod Agrippa (I) took over the new territory, he was apprehensive and wondered if his rule of law was going to be accepted amicably by the Jews that were in Jerusalem? To avoid discord and conflict, he went out of his way to reveal to them that he was observing the religious rules and traditions, which they had implemented. And to further show that he was on their side, Agrippa began to persecute and prosecute the apostles and the converts to Christianity. Eventually, he engrossed himself publicly by imprisoning and killing Apostle James, the son of Zebedee, by the sword.

The Apostles & Their Fate

Here are the references.

"1 Now about that time Herod the king stretched forth his hands to vex certain of the church.

"2 And he killed James the brother of John with the sword.

"3 And because he saw it pleased the Jews, he proceeded further to take Peter also. (Then were the days of unleavened bread.)." Acts 12:1-3

Apostle James the son of Zebedee was publicly executed by the sword, approximately ten years after Christ's resurrection took place. Apostle James' execution took place by the self-serving evil hand of King Agrippa (I) sometime between 41 AD and 44 AD. King Agrippa died in 44 AD from a violent sickness shortly after Apostle James' execution took place.

Andrew was, if I can use the word "was" under the circumstances, one of the twelve apostles and a brother of Simon Peter. According to Apostle John, Andrew was from the city of Bethsaida. John writes,

"44 Now Philip was of Bethsaida, the city of Andrew and Peter" (John 1:44).

Bethsaida was located on the northern shore of the Lake of Galilee. Apostle Andrew was a fisherman like his brother Simon Peter. We are told, "18 And Jesus, walking by the sea of Galilee, saw two brethren, Simon called Peter, and

The Apostles & Their Fate

Andrew his brother, casting a net into the sea: for they were fishers.

> "19 And He saith unto them, Follow Me, and I will make you fishers of men." Matthew 4:18, 19

Andrew was one of the two disciples to whom John the Baptist revealed, at the Jordan River, and pointed to Jesus as "the Lamb of God" (John 1:35-40).

And while the disciples were on the Mount of Olives, Andrew was one of the four disciples who collectively took Jesus aside from the group and asked Jesus privately to divulge what is the **"sign,"** which would reveal the coming destruction of Jerusalem. And, what is the "**sign**," which would reveal that Christ's 2nd coming is at hand?

The query of the "sign," which would reveal the destruction of Jerusalem and the Temple, surfaced after Jesus made the comment to His apostles that the Temple in Jerusalem would be totally destroyed to the ground by the Roman forces.

Here are the references.

"1 And as He went out of the temple, one of His disciples saith unto Him, Master, see what manner of stones and what buildings are here!

"2 And Jesus answering said unto him, Seest thou [you] these great buildings? there shall not be left one stone upon another, that shall not be thrown down.

"3 And as He sat upon the mount of Olives over against the temple, Peter and James and John and Andrew asked Him privately,

> "4 Tell us, when shall these things be? and what shall be the **sign** when all these things shall be

The Apostles & Their Fate

fulfilled?" Mark 13:1-4

In response to their inquiry, Jesus referred to the coming destruction of the Temple and Jerusalem by the pen of Luke in Luke 21. But, a reference to the destruction of the Temple and Jerusalem is not provided by Apostle John. And only Luke provides the description of the "sign" that was given by Jesus.

Jesus said,

> "20 And when ye [all of you] shall see Jerusalem compassed with armies, then know that the desolation thereof is nigh.

> "21 Then let them which are in Judaea flee to the mountains; and let them which are in the midst of it depart out; and let not them that are in the countries enter thereinto.

> "22 For these be the days of vengeance, that all things which are written may be fulfilled.

> "23 But woe unto them that are with child, and to them that give suck, in those days! for there shall be great distress in the land, and wrath upon this people.

> "24 And they shall fall by the edge of the sword, and shall be led away captive into all nations: and Jerusalem shall be trodden down of the Gentiles, until the times of the Gentiles be fulfilled." Luke 21:20-24

In the above verses Jesus in His mercy gives the description of the sign in verse twenty; and when the people in Jerusalem observe that they are surrounded by the Roman armies, they are to flee immediately for safety to the mountains and anywhere else except in the city of Jerusalem.

Unfortunately, the majority of the people in Jerusalem

The Apostles & Their Fate

did not take heed to Christ's and to the apostle's warning. And when the actual event took place, and the people of Jerusalem saw the Roman army retreat after it had surround Jerusalem, the people who took heed to the "sign" left Jerusalem and found safety throughout the region. Unfortunately, the struggle amongst the Jewish factions and hierarchy convinced the majority of the Jews to remain in Jerusalem and fight the Roman army. In doing so, through starvation, disease, and the onslaught without mercy by the Roman soldiers, in the spring of 70 AD, destroyed the two outer walls of Jerusalem, the Temple, the city of Jerusalem, and the majority of the Jewish population. And in regards to those individuals who did survive, some were taken to the arenas for sport and others were taken to slavery.

It did not have to be that way. If only the leaders of the House of Judah took heed to Christ's words, they would have spared the Temple, Jerusalem, and the people.

In addition, it should also be noted that Jesus spoke about a second **"sign."** It is recorded by Apostle Matthew.

Here are the references,

"1 And Jesus went out, and departed from the temple: and His disciples came to Him for to shew Him the buildings of the temple. 2 And Jesus said unto them, See ye [all of you] not all these things? verily I say unto you, There shall not be left here one stone upon another, that shall not be thrown down.

> "3 And as He sat upon the mount of Olives, the disciples came unto him privately, saying, Tell us, when shall these things be? and what shall be the **sign** of thy coming, and of the end of the world?" Matthew 24:1-3

The Apostles & Their Fate

In response to their query, if you were to read Mark thirteen, Luke twenty-one, and Matthew twenty-four, you will observe from Christ's statements, Jesus did not reveal to the four apostles the "sign" of Christ's 2nd coming, what the "sign" of Christ's 2nd coming looks like, where it will appear, and when it will precisely appear. You would think that such an important event would take precedence, and be revealed to the masses of the world, in order to make the public aware that Christ's 2nd coming is around the corner.

Instead, Christ the LORD of hosts tells His disciples after what massive event the "sign" would appear.

Here are His words,

> "29 Immediately after the tribulation of those days shall the sun be darkened, and the moon shall not give her light, and the stars shall fall from heaven, and the powers of the heavens shall be shaken:

> "30 And then shall appear the **sign** of the Son of man in heaven: and then shall all the tribes of the earth mourn, and they shall see the Son of man coming in the clouds of heaven with power and great glory." Matthew 24:29, 30

When is the "sign" of Christ's 2nd coming going to appear in heaven?

As per verse twenty-nine, the "sign" will appear right after the "great tribulation" of which we are living in; but, more precisely, "immediately" after "the heavens shall be shaken" (v. 29).

Nonetheless, although the "sign" of Christ's 2nd coming is not revealed or explained in the Gospels of Matthew, of Mark, of Luke, or of John, Matthew at least mentions it.

The Apostles & Their Fate

Although the "sign" was not revealed to the four apostles, on Mount Olives, a number of years later, about 95 AD, Apostle John was exiled to the Isle of Patmos for preaching the word of Jesus Christ the LORD (Revelation 1:9). And while he was in exile on the Isle of Patmos, the "sign" of Christ's 2nd coming was revealed to Apostle John.

Why was the "sign" not revealed in the four Gospels?

Why was the "sign" not revealed by the rest of the apostles?

Why was it tucked away in the book of Revelation?

Why was the "sign" not revealed to the world for the past 2,000 years?

And why is it revealed now, after 2,000 years?

The answer is simple; it was not the will of our heavenly Father to reveal it earlier.

Jesus confirms the above answer,

> "7 And He [Christ] said unto them [the apostles], It is not for you to know the times or the seasons, which the Father hath put in his own power." Acts 1:7

Today as you are reading this book, the "sign" of Christ's 2nd coming is been revealed to the masses of the world, just as the "great tribulation is revealed, and just as "the mark of the beast" is being revealed to the world. Nonetheless, the "sign" is described as to what it looks like, when it will appear, where it will appear, and how awesome and massive it will be; in fact, not a single person on planet earth will miss it.

For more information on the "sign" of Christ's 2nd coming, the revelation of what the "sign" looks like, who will see it, how big it is, when it will appear, and where it will appear, please read my book called *"The Sign in Matthew 24"* By: Philip Mitanidis BEEHIVE PUBLISHING HOUSE INC.

The Apostles & Their Fate

Nonetheless, going back to Apostle Andrew; after the resurrection of Jesus Christ our LORD God and Savior, Andrew can be found in Jerusalem, in the upper room, interacting with the other ten disciples (Acts 1:13, 14).

But, in regards to his fate, like many of the Apostles of Christ, Scripturally, nothing is known with certainty of Andrew's later life and where he preached the Gospel last. But, tradition asserts that he is said to have preached the Gospel of Jesus Christ (Mark 1:1) all the way to Scotland, in Scythia, and in Thrace, which is in the northern part of Greece. And while he was in Greece, he was captured and martyred there. Tradition also has it that Apostle Andrew, the brother of Simon Peter, was crucified in Greece on an X-shaped cross, for that reason it is called the St. Andrew's cross.

Philip the apostle is commonly confused with Philip the deacon who is spoken of in the book of Acts. Philip is one of the twelve apostles. His home was in Bethsaida (John 1:44), which was in the northern shore of the Sea of Galilee. Philip was first attracted to the message of John the Baptist; and through John the Baptist, he was one of the early apostles to be attracted to Jesus as the Messiah, as "the Lamb of God," and the acceptance of Jesus as his LORD God and Savior.

Philip was the one who brought Nathanael to Jesus (John 1:45-51). About a year and a half later, he was one of the twelve men who were ordained as apostles of Jesus Christ the LORD (Matthew 10:2-5).

Later on in the year, prior to feeding the 5,000, Apostle Philip ran into a big obstacle; how was he going to feed 5,000 people? Therefore he questioned Jesus' command to feed the 5,000 people. Philip said to Jesus, "Whence shall we buy bread, that these may eat?" (John 6:5).

And near the end of Christ's ministry, Philip asked Jesus to "8 shew us the Father, and it suficeth us" (John 14:8).

The Apostles & Their Fate

"9 Jesus saith unto him, Have I been so long time with you, and yet hast thou [you] not known me, Philip? he that hath seen me hath seen the Father; and how sayest thou [you] then, Shew us the Father? 10 Believest thou [you] not that I am in the Father, and the Father in me? the words that I speak unto you I speak not of myself: but the Father that dwelleth in me, he doeth the works. 11 Believe me that I am in the Father, and the Father in me: or else believe me for the very works' sake." John 14:8-11

After Christ's resurrection, Apostle Philip can be seen, prior to Pentecost, in the upper room in Jerusalem (Acts 1:13), with the other apostles and with the other believers in Christ.

Beside the record of "The Gospel According to John," nothing more is known about Apostle Philip.

Traditionally, it is believed that Apostle Philip preached mostly in the area of Phrygia in Asia Minor.

Nathanael (Bartholomew), can be seen amongst the other apostles by the name of "Nathanael of Cana," as in the following verse.

"2 There were together Simon Peter, and Thomas called Didymus, and Nathanael of Cana in Galilee, and the [sons] of Zebedee, and two other of his disciples." (John 21:2)

But, Apostle "Nathanael of Cana in Galilee" can also be seen amongst the apostles by the name of Bartholomew (v.3), as in the following verses.

"2 Now the names of the twelve apostles are these; The first, Simon, who is called Peter, and Andrew his brother; James the son of Zebedee, and John his brother;

The Apostles & Their Fate

"3 Philip, and Bartholomew; Thomas, and Matthew the publican; James the son of Alphaeus, and Lebbaeus, whose surname was Thaddaeus;

"4 Simon the Canaanite, and Judas Iscariot, who also betrayed Him." Matthew 10:2-5

Nathanael, a native of Galilee, was brought by Philip to Jesus for his consideration to see if He was the Messiah or not. In doing so, Nathanael found it hard to believe that the Messiah would be living in such a disreputable town as Nazareth (John 1:46). But after meeting Jesus and talking with Him, Nathanael exclaimed,

"49 Nathanael answered and saith unto Him [Jesus], Rabbi, thou [You] art the Son of God; thou [You] art the King of Israel." John 1:49

Jesus left such an overwhelming impression upon Nathanael, like Philip, he too accepted Jesus to be "the Messiah," "the Son of God," "the King of Israel," and as his LORD God and Savior.

And, as per tradition, Nathanael (Bartholomew) is believed to have preached the Gospel of Jesus in Arabia, Ethiopia, Armenia, and perhaps in the lands adjoining those areas. Although there is no Scriptural evidence of Nathanael's death; as per tradition, it is believed that Nathanael was crucified head downward to the ground in one of the provinces of Armenia.

Matthew is often referred to by the name of Levi.

Although apostles Luke and Mark refer to Matthew by the name of Levi, Mark also identifies Matthew as the son of

The Apostles & Their Fate

Alphaeus.

Here are the references:

> "27 And after these things He [Christ] went forth, and saw a publican, named Levi, sitting at the receipt of custom: and He said unto him, Follow me." Luke 5:27

> "14 And as He passed by, He saw Levi the son of Alphaeus sitting at the receipt of custom, and said unto him, Follow me. And he arose and followed Him." Mark 2:14

Levi Matthew was a tax collector ("publican") employed in the service of Herod Antipas' political office. He was stationed in the city of Capernaum (Matthew 9:9), which is located in the northern shore of the Sea of Galilee. He listened to Christ's Gospel message with sincere interest; and when he was called by Jesus to follow Him, Matthew relinquished his job as a tax collector and became one of Christ's twelve disciples (Matthew 10:2, 3).

Moreover, it is commonly agreed that Matthew the Levi wrote by his hand the Gospel "According to Matthew" in the Greek language prior to the destruction of Jerusalem in 70 AD. And the internal evidence of the Gospel "According to Matthew" reveals from the Old Testament (OT) that the Messianic prophecies were fulfilled by Jesus Christ the LORD God of Israel.

Nonetheless, Matthew in his later years, it appears that he devoted most of his time revealing the Gospel of Jesus Christ the LORD God of Abraham to the defiant Jewish authorities that resided in the city of Jerusalem. Beyond that, noticeable, as per Scripture, nothing further is known as to when and where his labors ended, with the exception of

The Apostles & Their Fate

what tradition has to say; it places him in Parthia, Palestine, and Persia and suggests that he did not suffer martyrdom.

Thomas, also called Didymus, is revealed by Matthew, Mark, and Luke as one of the twelve ordained apostles. And Apostle John reveals some of the events that surrounded Thomas.

John speaks of the time when Martha and Mary, sisters of their dead brother Lazarus, requested, before Lazarus died, for Jesus to come and heal him. But Jesus purposely tarried and did not go to see him right away. Eventually, Jesus said to His disciples that He would go to see him. But because twice prior to Lazarus' death, the Jews in Jerusalem picked up stones to stone Jesus (John 8:59; 10:31), Thomas did not want anyone to go there. Fearing that they might finally capture Jesus and stone Him to death, Thomas tried to discourage everybody in the group from going to Jerusalem, in order to avoid their demise. But the final decision was made by Jesus to go to Jerusalem and see His dead friend Lazarus.

Hearing Jesus' decision,

"16 Then said Thomas, which is called Didymus, unto his fellowdisciples, Let us also go, that we may die with Him." John 11:16

And, as you probably already know, Jesus did resurrect Lazarus even though he was in the grave for four days. (Read John chapter eleven for the details.)

In the night, prior to Christ's betrayal by Judas Iscariot with a "kiss," Jesus took the time to explain to the disciples His death, resurrection, and ascension. Thomas not seeking clarity to Christ's statements of His ascension, misunderstood what Jesus was saying; consequently, Thomas made an unrelated remark to the subject matter of Christ's presentation by saying,

The Apostles & Their Fate

> "5 unto Him, LORD, we know not whither thou [You] goest; and how can we know the way?" (John 14:5).

In another incident, before Christ's ascension took place, to the third heaven, early on Sunday morning, near the sepulcher, Jesus appeared to Mary, and when she realized who He was, she went to embrace Him; but, "17 Jesus saith unto her, Touch me not; for I am not yet ascended to my Father" (John 20:17). After Jesus finished speaking with Mary, He ascended to God the Father in the third heaven; and after a brief stay, Jesus returned to the earth and appeared to many of the disciples during their diverse travels, in order to show them that He was alive and to expound some of the Scriptures, which they did not understand.

In another occasion, Jesus appeared to the disciples in the upper room; but at that time, Thomas was not there. After eight days, Thomas arrived in the upper room. Then the disciples told Thomas that Jesus had come to visit them. But, Thomas did not believe them. He said,

> "25 Except I shall see in His hands the print of the nails, and put my finger into the print of the nails, and thrust my hand into His side, I will not believe.

Well, Thomas got his wish because, "26 after eight days again His disciples were within, and Thomas with them: then came Jesus, the doors being shut, and stood in the midst, and said, Peace be unto you.

"27 Then saith He to Thomas, Reach hither thy finger, and behold my hands; and reach hither thy [your] hand, and thrust it into my side: and be not faithless, but believing.

The Apostles & Their Fate

"28 And Thomas answered and said unto Him, My LORD and My God.

"29 Jesus saith unto him, Thomas, because thou [you] hast seen Me, thou [you] hast believed: blessed are they that have not seen, and yet have believed." John 20:25-29

Tradition assigns Thomas to Parthia and Persia, and in his later years to Edessa, where he is said to have been martyred.

However, there is also another tradition, which claims that Apostle Thomas preached the Gospel of Jesus Christ the LORD (Mark 1:1) in southern India. A place near Madras, India; it is called St. Thomas' Mount. There is a Monastery and a group of Christian believers residing outside of the Monastery, which call themselves the Thomas Christians.

On the other hand some claim that the likelihood is that Thomas' labors did not reach that far.

But, then again, we can ask, why not?

He could be one of the disciples Jesus referred to who is still alive today? Consequently, he could be the one who preached in India, in China, in the Philippines, and in other parts of the world?

Simon the zealot (Simon the Canaanite of v.4 below) was chosen by Jesus as one of the twelve apostles.

Here is one reference:

"2 Now the names of the twelve apostles are these; The first, Simon, who is called Peter, and Andrew his brother; James the son of Zebedee, and John his brother; 3 Philip, and Bartholomew; Thomas, and Matthew the

The Apostles & Their Fate

> publican; James the son of Alphaeus, and
> Lebbaeus, whose surname was Thaddaeus; 4
> Simon the Canaanite, and Judas Iscariot, who
> also betrayed Him." Matthew 10:2-4

Apostle "Simon the Canaanite" is also identified by
Apostle Luke by the name of "Simon the Zelotes." (See Luke
6:13-16; and Acts 1:13.)

Here is one of the references:

> "13 And when they were come in, they went up
> into an upper room, where abode both Peter,
> and James, and John, and Andrew, Philip, and
> Thomas, Bartholomew, and Matthew, James the
> son of Alphaeus, and Simon Zelotes, and Judas
> the brother of James." Acts 1:13

The Bible prophets do not disclose a lot more beyond
the above observation. For that reason, it kind of begs the
question, why not?

But, there is a tradition, which claims that Simon the
Zelote labored mostly in the region of North Africa. And yet,
we are told that he was martyred in Palestine during the reign
of the Roman Emperor Domitian, who was bent on
persecuting the Christians. It is also believed that during that
time, Domitian also exiled Apostle John to the barren volcanic
Isle of Patmos that is located in the Aegean Sea.

James (Son of Alphaeus) is one of the twelve apostles
who was ordained by Jesus; but he, at the first glance, like
Matthew creates a little bit of confusion for us as to who he is?

His identity is confusing because the 2nd James in
Luke's list (Luke 6:13-16) is identified as the son of a man
called "Alphaeus."

The Apostles & Their Fate

Here is the reference:

"13 And when it was day, He called unto Him His disciples: and of them He chose twelve, whom also He named apostles; 14 Simon, (whom he also named Peter,) and Andrew his brother, James and John, Philip and Bartholomew, 15 Matthew and Thomas, James the son of Alphaeus, and Simon called Zelotes, 16 And Judas the brother of James, and Judas Iscariot, which also was the traitor." Luke 6:13-16

But, Matthew, who is also identified by the name of "Levi," is said to be "the son of Alphaeus."
Here is the account:

"14 And as He passed by, He saw Levi the son of Alphaeus sitting at the receipt of custom, and said unto him, Follow Me. And he arose and followed Him." Mark 2:14

And Levi, the custom officer, is identified by the name of Matthew.

"9 And as Jesus passed forth from thence, He saw a man, named Matthew, sitting at the receipt of custom: and He saith unto him, Follow Me. And he arose, and followed Him." Matthew 9:9

And, to complicate matters even more, we are told by Luke, "Judas is the brother of James" (The 2nd James in the above list of Luke 6:13-16).

The Apostles & Their Fate

Although it can be confusing, if you are not paying attention to what is being said by the prophets of Christ the LORD, we can conclude from the above references, Judas is the brother of the 2nd James; and the 2nd James is the brother of Levi Matthew. Or, simplistically, we can also conclude that the name "Alphaeus" refers to two separate individuals; and if that is the case, we can also conclude that Levi Matthew is not the brother of the two brothers, the 2nd James on the apostles' list, and his brother Judas.

There is not much more that can be said about the 2nd James, beyond that, we know very little. Scripturally, we do not know if he is still alive today or if he is dead?

Judas (Lebbaeus Thaddaeus). Judas the brother of the 2nd James on the list of the apostles is one of the twelve apostles Jesus appointed. We know that Judas is also identified by the name of "Lebbaeus, whose sir name was Thaddaeus" because Apostle's Matthew and Mark identify him as such.

Here are the references

"2 Now the names of the twelve apostles are these; The first, Simon, who is called Peter, and Andrew his brother; James the son of Zebedee, and John his brother; 3 Philip, and Bartholomew; Thomas, and Matthew the publican; James the son of Alphaeus, and Lebbaeus, whose surname was Thaddaeus; 4 Simon the Canaanite, and Judas Iscariot, who also betrayed Him." Matthew 10:2-4

"15 And to have power to heal sicknesses, and to cast out devils: 16 And Simon He surnamed Peter; 17 And James the son of Zebedee, and John the brother of James; and He surnamed them Boanerges, which is, The sons of thunder: 18 And Andrew, and Philip, and

The Apostles & Their Fate

Bartholomew, and Matthew, and Thomas, and James the son of Alphaeus, and Thaddaeus, and Simon the Canaanite, 19 And Judas Iscariot, which also betrayed Him: and they went into an house." Mark 3:15-19

And, notably, you will also find that Apostle John carefully distinguishes between Judah the brother of the 2nd James on the List (Luke 6: 13-16) to Judas Iscariot.

Here is the account:

"22 Judas saith unto Him, not Iscariot, LORD, how is it that thou [You] wilt manifest thyself unto us, and not unto the world?" (John 14:22).

Therefore the Judas that is referred to in the lists of Luke 6:13-16 and Acts 1:13 is the individuals who is also identified by the name of "Lebbaeus, whose surname is Thaddaeus" in the lists of Matthew 10:2-5 and Mark 3:15-19.

And, as far as Judas Iscariot is concerned, who betrayed Jesus with a "kiss," he is identified at the bottom of the lists with the exception of Acts 1:13.

*   If you want to compare the lists of the twelve apostles by the three apostles, here are the references: Matthew 10:2-5; Mark 3:15-19; Luke 6:13-16; and Acts 1:13:

Matthias, according to the record of the first chapter of Acts, was chosen by God the Holy Ghost to fill the vacancy left by Judas Iscariot who betrayed Jesus Christ to the evil hands of the priests and elders of the Jewish people.

The record states, by the mouth of Apostle Peter,

"16 Men and brethren, this scripture must needs have been fulfilled, which the Holy Ghost by the mouth of

The Apostles & Their Fate

David spake before concerning Judas, which was guide to them that took Jesus. 17 For he was numbered with us, and had obtained part of this ministry.

"18 Now this man purchased a field with the reward of iniquity; and falling headlong, he burst asunder in the midst, and all his bowels gushed out.

"19 And it was known unto all the dwellers at Jerusalem; insomuch as that field is called in their proper tongue, Aceldama, that is to say, The field of blood.

"20 For it is written in the book of Psalms, Let his habitation be desolate, and let no man dwell therein: and his bishoprick let another take.

"21 Wherefore of these men which have companied with us all the time that the LORD Jesus went in and out among us, 22 Beginning from the baptism of John, unto that same day that He was taken up from us, must one be ordained to be a witness with us of his resurrection.

"23 And they appointed two, Joseph called Barsabas, who was surnamed Justus, and Matthias.

"24 And they prayed, and said, Thou [You], LORD, which knowest the hearts of all men, shew whether of these two thou [You] hast chosen, 25 That he may take part of this ministry and apostleship, from which Judas by transgression fell, that he might go to his own place.

"26 And they gave forth their lots; and the lot fell upon Matthias; and he was numbered with the eleven apostles." Acts 1:16-26

Although God the Holy Spirit chose Matthias to be one of the twelve apostles of Jesus Christ the LORD, it is believed that Matthias was one of the seventy followers of Christ whom Christ appointed and sent out two by two (Luke 10:1) to preach the Gospel.

It is said that Apostle Matthias had preached in Cappadocia, north of Apostle Paul's home province of Cilicia.

On the other hand, tradition attests that Apostle Matthias was martyred somewhere in the province of Judea.

Peter is one of the twelve ordained apostles. He is first identified by the name of Simon, and the son of Jona. But as far as the name of "Peter" is concerned, Jesus gave him that name when his brother Andrew first brought him to Jesus. (See John 1:40-42.) Peter was a resident of the city of Bethsaida located on the northeastern shore of the Sea of Galilee. He was married (Matthew 8:14), and was a fisherman by trade. Peter was one of the four Apostles who had the privilege of being with Jesus during the Transfiguration (Matthew 17:1), and in Gethsemane (Mark 14:33). Peter openly confessed Jesus to be the Messiah, and the Son of God (Matthew 16:16); and yet, after Jesus Christ was seized by the Jewish authority, Peter also permitted to be intimidated by the bystanders and those who said to him that he was one of the disciples of Jesus Christ. And through that intimidation, Peter sinned three times (He broke the Ten Commandments 3 times. See Exodus 20:16; 1 John 3:4). By denying Christ openly three times to his accusers, Peter fulfilled Christ's words to the letter. (See Matthew 26:33, 34.)

After receiving the power of God the Holy Spirit in the upper room, Peter gave a stunning sermon, which impressed over 3,000 people to convert to Christianity. (See Acts 2:14-41.)

The Apostles & Their Fate

Later, when John and Peter were at the Gate Beautiful, Peter healed a lame man. The Jewish authorities did not like to hear that the man was healed in the name of Jesus Christ and therefore arrested them. And when brought before the Sanhedrin Peter again preached Christ. And when Peter and John were told by the Jewish authorities not to preach in the name of Jesus Christ, they responded by saying that they cannot deny what they have seen and heard about Jesus Christ the LORD.

Here is the account:

"18 And they called them, and commanded them not to speak at all nor teach in the name of Jesus.

"19 But Peter and John answered and said unto them, Whether it be right in the sight of God to hearken unto you more than unto God, judge ye.

"20 For we cannot but speak the things which we have seen and heard.

"21 So when they had further threatened them, they let them go, finding nothing how they might punish them, because of the people: for all men glorified God for that which was done.

"22 For the man was above forty years old, on whom this miracle of healing was shewed.

"23 And being let go, they went to their own company, and reported all that the chief priests and elders had said unto them." Acts 4:18-23.

After that, while they were at the Temple, they were surrounded with a large throng of people, Peter again testified of the death, and resurrection, and the power in the name of

The Apostles & Their Fate

Jesus Christ the God of Israel. (See Acts 3:12-26.)

Furthermore, the LORD gave Peter a vision, while he was staying at Simon's house. And in that vision the LORD told Peter not to call any man "common or unclean" (Acts 10:9-17, 28). Peter returned to Jerusalem and was asked to explain his association with the Gentiles in harmony with the Scriptures. (See Acts 11:1-18.); and while in Jerusalem Peter was once more imprisoned; but the angel of Jesus Christ the LORD released Peter from his shackles. (See Acts 12:1-11.)

A lot more can be said about Apostle Peter; but in closing, it is said by some that Peter died a Martyr. In fact, according to tradition, Peter was crucified head downward to the ground in the year of 67 AD. But, according to Scripture, Peter was to die of old age. So! Who are you going to believe, Scripture or tradition?

John an apostle of Jesus Christ is the son of Zebedee, and the brother of the executed Apostle James.

Here is the reference to confirm that fact:

> "21 And going on from thence, He [Christ] saw other two brethren, James the son of Zebedee, and John his brother, in a ship with Zebedee their father, mending their nets; and He called them.

> "22 And they immediately left the ship and their father, and followed Him." Matthew 4:21

Moreover, as the above verses indicate, John, his father Zebedee, and James his brother were fishermen by trade, and apparently reasonable prosperous (Mark 1:19, 20). In fact, they were all in partnership with Peter and Andrew.

Apostle John wrote the "Gospel According to John,"

The Apostles & Their Fate

the Book of Revelation, and the three letters (The 1st Epistle of John, The 2nd Epistle of John, and The 3rd Epistle of John). All of these writings can be found in the (NT). And, as the titles indicate, they are identified by his name.

Oddly, Apostle John entered the Gospel narrative in John 1:35-40, as an unnamed disciple; and ends "The Gospel According to John" the same way!

John was mingling among the multitude, interacting with the multitude, and listening intently to the words of the Baptist who was preaching, by the Jordan River, of the coming Messiah. From John's narrative, it appears that Andrew, Peter's brother, and John the son of Zebedee were the first of John the Baptist's disciples to follow Jesus.

John returned with Jesus to Galilee. Three days later Jesus and His early apostles were invited to attend the wedding festivities at Cana (John 2:1-11) where they observed the second miracle.

John was with Jesus Christ intermittently during the Galilean ministry and during the Judean ministry, which followed. But, as Jesus began His Galilean ministry again, He called Peter, Andrew, John, and James to follow Him (Luke 5:1-11). Few months later on, Peter, Andrew, John, and James were among the twelve men that were chosen by Jesus to be apostles (Matthew 10:2). From that time forward, Apostle John was closely associated with Jesus Christ his LORD in his labors.

Apostle John witnessed the resurrection of Jairus' daughter (Mark 5:37). He was present at the Transfiguration (Mark 9:2), and again at Gethsemane (Mark 14:33-42). On Sunday morning, John ran to the sepulcher to see if Jesus had risen.

And in regards to his character, John gave evidence of an impulsive disposition upon various occasions. As an example, he wanted to bring fire upon the Samaritan village

The Apostles & Their Fate

because they would not receive Jesus and His disciples (Luke 9:52-56). John, his brother, and his mother revealed their selfish attitude when they sought a place next to Jesus (Matthew 20:20-24; Mark 10:35-41). On the other hand, Apostle John displayed enthusiasm and loyalty by his willingness to die for Jesus Christ his LORD and for Christ's Gospel.

When Jesus was arrested in Gethsemane, John followed Jesus into the palace of the high priest (John 18:15); and later to Calvary (John 19:26, 27). At the cross Jesus entrusted His mother Mary to the loving care of John (John 19:26, 27).

And, early Sunday morning,

"1 The first day of the week cometh Mary Magdalene early, when it was yet dark, unto the sepulchre, and seeth the stone taken away from the sepulchre. 2 Then she runneth, and cometh to Simon Peter, and to the other disciple [John], whom Jesus loved, and saith unto them, They have taken away the LORD out of the sepulchre, and we know not where they have laid him.

"3 Peter therefore went forth, and that other disciple [John], and came to the sepulchre. 4 So they ran both together: and the other disciple did outrun Peter, and came first to the sepulchre. 5 And he stooping down, and looking in, saw the linen clothes lying; yet went he not in.

"6 Then cometh Simon Peter following him, and went into the sepulchre, and seeth the linen clothes lie, 7 And the napkin, that was about his head, not lying with the linen clothes, but wrapped together in a place by itself.

"8 Then went in also that other disciple [John], which came first to the sepulchre, and he saw, and believed."

The Apostles & Their Fate

John 20:1-8

After Christ's ascension to heaven, Apostle John remained with the other ten apostles and with others in the upper room, in one of the houses, in the city of Jerusalem (Acts 1:13). Later, John joined with Peter in missionary work throughout the city of Jerusalem (Acts 3:1). Even though both apostles experienced imprisonment, they witnessed courageously to their faith in the Messiah (Christ, John 1:41) (Acts 4:19). Later, they went to Samaria to help Philip with his missionary work (Acts 8:14). John was among the "apostles and elders which were at Jerusalem" for a number of years (Acts 16:4; Galatians 2:9).

Assumingly, by the implication in Revelation 1:11, tradition suggests Apostle John's headquarters was moved from Jerusalem to Ephesus and was in charge of the seven churches in the Roman province of Asia Minor. From there he was banished by Emperor Domitian to the island of Patmos for preaching the word of God (Revelation 1:9); but, he is thought to have been released during the time when Nerva became emperor of the Roman Empire in 96 AD. Following his release, according to tradition, and contrary to Scripture, it is said that Apostle John resided at Ephesus, and died during the reign of Trojan, some time between 98 AD to 117 AD.

Nonetheless, as you have noted in each foregoing brief presentation, of the twelve apostles of Jesus Christ the LORD, very little information is given to us about them; and in regards to the demise of the majority of the apostles. As you have noted, the information is absent from their written records, which they have presented to us.

Therefore, it is important to note that the apostles were inspired to preach and write the Gospel message of Jesus Christ (Romans 1:9, 16; Mark 1:1) instead of concentrating on their personal lives, outcome, and death.

The Apostles & Their Fate

It should also be noted, the apostles who oversaw the affairs of the Christian church, from the city of Jerusalem, knew where the apostles were in the mission field. Therefore, if it was the will of God the Holy Spirit to disclose the death of every apostle, they would have done it (2 Timothy 3:16; 2 Peter 1:19-21). But, the very fact that they did not disclose the death of every apostle speaks very loud that there was a reason why they did not reveal where they were at a given time, and what happened to them? In fact, as you probably already observed, there is hardly any information regarding the majority of the twelve ordained apostles.

Although the twelve apostles appear out of sight and out of mind because of lack of information, they do appear collectively in "the prophecy" of the book of Revelation, one more time, exalted by naming the twelve pillars of the foundation of the heavenly Jerusalem by their respective names.

Here is the reference:

"14 And the wall of the city had twelve foundations, and in them the names of the twelve apostles of the Lamb [Jesus Christ]." Revelation 21:14

So! Why is there, in the sixty-six books of the Bible, such a shortage of information on the seventy disciples and on the twelve ordained apostles?

It appears from the record, the majority of the apostles kept their exposures and deaths a secret in order to protect the identity of the apostles who are still alive today in our world. By not exposing the apostles who are still alive today, it has protected them from exposure to wicked ungodly hands, persecution, hounding, singling out, ridicule, scorn, derision, harassment, stalking, pestering, defamation of character,

The Apostles & Their Fate

misrepresentation, exhibitionism, exploitation, starvation, torture, death, etc., etc.

On the other hand, you would think that the historians, influenced by tradition, would have some of the truth, if not the whole truth, as to when each apostle was pronounced dead or alive at any given time and where?

Obviously tradition has failed to provide the information.

Unfortunately, traditionalist and historians assumed to a large degree, since man on an average dies at the age of seventy-five, the apostles would have died at that age and probably at the last known location, and therefore reported their outcome as such.

But, perceptibly, the silence of the apostle's longevity, before they embark openly upon their public mission for the second time, and testify before kindred, tongues, and nations, has been a secret for the past 2,000 years. Now, their existence is revealed, just like the "sign" in Matthew 24:30 is being revealed, and just like the "mark of the beast" is being revealed (Rev. 13:18), and just as the "great tribulation" is revealed.

The fact that Scripturally, the word "some" is used to state that there is more than one apostle to remain alive until Jesus comes "in His kingdom," we can conclude that there is more than one apostle who has remained alive and is with us today. But, that Scriptural fact poses a number of questions.

Why was their longevity kept a secret for the past 2,000 years?

Why are these facts, after 2,000 years revealed to us now?

Is it time for the apostles to surface and "prophesy again before many peoples, and nations, and tongues, and kings," is that why?

And, when they do, what are they going to say to us verbally that they could not say or can't say by the written

The Apostles & Their Fate

word?

It must be of immense importance that their message or messages have to be given personally and verbally to the human race?

And we can also ask, how are they going to be received by the masses of the world, especially by those who hate Christ the LORD (Exodus 20:5) and His messengers?

And when Satan personally gets involved and kills the apostles, why would the wicked unrepentant men and women be celebrating their deaths, and giving gifts to each other?

What do you think?

Are there answers?

The Apostles & Their Fate

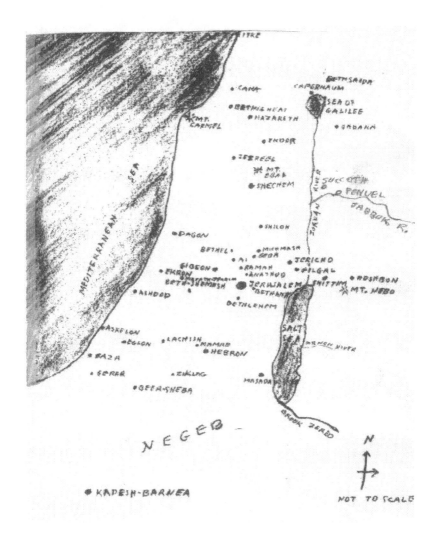

The Book of
Revelation an Overview

Up until few years ago, the book of Revelation (of the Bible) and its subject matter of its prophecy were deemed incomprehensible by the Muslims, Jews, Christians, and others. Therefore, it was not relentlessly attacked on its doctrinal foundation as the other Gospel books of the Bible were and are still attacked today. And the reason the attacks were not as severe on the book of Revelation was due to the fact that most of the theologians, clergy, and laymen of these religious institutions had concluded that the book of Revelation is mostly figurative; and therefore it poses a real problem for the reader of the book to know the meaning of its symbolism or to understand its message or to come to some conclusion or to bring closure to "the prophecy." Consequently, their opinions, which still exist today, are aligned with some of the inconclusive popular doctrinal beliefs of the churches that are based upon the book of Revelation.

Therefore, the above begs the question?

Is the book of Revelation, in its present form, hard to understand?

Is that the reason why the angel of Jesus Christ the LORD of hosts said to Apostle John,

> "11 Thou [you] must prophesy again before
> many peoples, and nations, and tongues, and
> kings"? Revelation 10:11

Or, is it because people do not understand the symbols in the book, or is it because of what Apostle John wrote in the book of Revelation.

The Book of Revelation an Overview

If those are the few reasons, we can ask, why did he write the book in that form, in the first place?

Obviously there was a reason why "the prophecy" of the book of Revelation had to be concealed; and the reason why it was written in its present form. The "prophecy" was hid from the enemies of Jesus Christ the LORD until such time God the Father deemed it appropriate to reveal (Acts 1:7) "the prophecy," and allow it to take its course. The revelation of "the prophecy" was to be revealed throughout the world during the time when Satan, his evil angels, and his satanic agencies try to hinder the three angel's messages of Revelation 14:6-9 of the prophecy. But, more aggressively upon the messages of the first angel, which says,

"6 And I saw another angel fly in the midst of heaven, having the everlasting gospel to preach unto them that dwell on the earth, and to every nation, and kindred, and tongue, and people,

"7 Saying with a loud voice, Fear God, and give glory to Him; for the hour of His judgment is come: and worship Him [Christ] that made heaven, and earth, and the sea, and the fountains of waters." Revelation 14:6, 7

As you have read, the first angel is to preach through willing hands with a loud voice to "Fear God, and give glory to Him;" and to warn the people of planet earth, "for the hour of His judgment is come:" and to direct the people to "worship Him [Christ: Nehemiah 9:6, 7; Colossians 1:16] that made heaven, and earth, and the sea, and the fountains of waters."

The Book of Revelation an Overview

But, by trying to stop the spread of the above three messages, Satan and his satanic agencies, in effect, would be helping to reveal the three angel's messages by their actions and bring "the prophecy" to conclusion.

And because Satan and his satanic agencies, today, are trying very hard to hinder the fulfillment of Revelation 14:6-7, and the rest of the "prophecy" of the book of Revelation, after 2,000 years, it is already being revealed; and it is spreading throughout the world as you are reading this book.

But because the "prophecy" reveals the last events of the earth's history and who is behind all of the evil atrocities that are imposed upon men, women, children, animals, and upon the ecosystem of the earth, Satan is spinning propaganda through his worshippers to discourage people from reading the book of Revelation. In fact, Satan has gone to the lengths of telling people throughout his satanic agencies that the book of Revelation is forbidden to read.

So! Why am I making such a statement?

I am making the above statement because, it should be noted that it is Satan, Satan's evil angels, men, and women, who hate Jesus Christ the LORD of hosts (Exodus 20:5), they are the ones behind all of the atrocities in the world. They are the ones who do not want to repent, and neither do they want to lose planet earth as their home, or be burnt to ashes (Malachi 4:1-3). Instead they want to exterminate all of Christ's penitent people from the face of the earth, claim the earth for themselves as their sovereign place amongst the other planets of the universe, and live in sin on earth in anarchy with Satan as their god and be possessed by his evil angels to do their bidding. Therefore, they are unleashing the gates of unrestrained evil carnage upon the world as far as their imagination can take them. They are seeking to impose the events of Revelation 13:11-18 by law upon Christ's penitent people, in order to deter them from accepting Jesus Christ as

The Book of Revelation an Overview

their LORD God and Savior. And, if they are not deterred, and do not conform to their evil wishes, the death penalty will be imposed upon them by civil law.

Here is the reference:

> "15 And he [2nd beast (v.11): England &
> America] had power to give life unto the image
> of the beast [1st beast (pope), vs. 1-10] that the
> image of the beast should both speak, and cause
> that as many as would not worship the image
> [the pope's pagan religious and political
> doctrine] of the beast should be killed."
> Revelation 13:15

As you have noted, thus far, I have unfolded for you few prophetic events from "the prophecy" (Revelation 1:3) of the book of Revelation to show you that the book of Revelation is not hard to understand its symbols or its writings (Revelation 22:10), which exist in the present form. But, if you need more information read my book called *"What is the Sign of Thy Coming and the End of the World"* By: Philip Mitanidis

Therefore the book of Revelation is not incomprehensible or hard to understand when its prophetic message is revealed by God the Holy Spirit to the penitent sinner. In fact, the book of Revelation and its doctrinal message is like any other doctrinal message of the sixty-five books of the Bible. You and I would not be able to understand the doctrinal message of the sixty-six books of the Bible if God the Christ, God the Holy Spirit, or God the Father would not give us the ability to understand what we are reading. If the veil or fog from our mind's eye is not removed from the word of the LORD, we can read and read and read till dooms day, and we would still not be able to understand the true meaning of His word.

The Book of Revelation an Overview

As an example, Jesus said to Peter,

"17 Blessed art thou [you], Simon Barjona: for flesh and blood hath not revealed it unto thee [you], but my Father which is in heaven." Matthew 16:17

Likewise, if God the Holy Spirit did not reveal Jesus Christ the Messiah (John 1:41) to "Simeon," he would have been waiting forever and would have missed Him even if He were to pass by him or speak to him. We are told:

"25 And, behold, there was a man in Jerusalem, whose name was Simeon; and the same man was just and devout, waiting for the consolation of Israel: and the Holy Ghost was upon him.

"26 And it was revealed unto him by the Holy Ghost, that he should not see death, before he had seen the Lord's Christ." Luke 2:25, 26

Jesus also admonished His apostles by saying to them,

"11 when they bring you unto the synagogues, and unto magistrates, and powers, take ye [all of you] no thought how or what thing ye shall answer, or what ye shall say:

"12 For the Holy Ghost shall teach you in the same hour what ye ought to say." Luke 12:11, 12

Apostle Paul the Benjamite also acknowledged the above verses, without the guidance of God the Holy Spirit, he would not have known and understood the Gospel of Jesus Christ the LORD. In fact, he even tells the Ephesians that it is by the power of the Holy Spirit "when ye read, ye [all of you] may understand my knowledge in the mystery of Christ)."

Here are the references:

"1 For this cause I Paul, the prisoner of Jesus Christ for you Gentiles, 2 If ye [all of you] have heard of the dispensation of the grace of God which is given me to you-ward:

"3 How that by revelation he made known unto me the mystery; (as I wrote afore in few words,

"4 Whereby, when ye [all of you] read, ye may understand my knowledge in the mystery of Christ)

"5 Which in other ages was not made known unto the sons of men, as it is now revealed unto His holy apostles and prophets by the Spirit." Ephesians 3:1-5

Apostle Paul in the above verses says, "4 the mystery of Christ) 5 Which in other ages was not made known unto the sons of men," now is revealed by the power of the "Spirit."

Prior to Christ's coming in the flesh "the mystery of Christ" was not revealed because without Christ's supreme sacrifice on Calvary's cross, grace, forgiveness, and the mystery of Christ would have non-effect upon the sinner. But now, we can understand by the will of God the Holy Spirit the grace of Jesus Christ, the forgiveness of our sins, the death of Jesus Christ on Calvary's cross, and the mystery of Jesus Christ the LORD God of His universe.

Therefore, we can conclude, it is by the will of God the Christ, by God the Father, but mainly by God the Holy Spirit a

The Book of Revelation an Overview

person is made to understand the writings of the Bible, and that includes the humongous prophetic events of "the prophecy" found in the book of Revelation.

But, like the other books of the Bible, the book of Revelation is a very special book. As soon as you start reading it, you receive a blessing from Jesus Christ the LORD God of Abraham. And, if you are a penitent sinner and you want to do the will of Jesus Christ, God the Holy Spirit will give you sufficient understanding of "the prophecy," when you first start to read the book until such time, like the brethren in Christ, you fully understand "the testimony of Jesus."

It is evident that you will know and understand "the prophecy," which is in the book of Revelation because God the Holy Spirit, looking forward to the time when "the time is at hand" (Rev. 1:3) is to reveal "the prophecy," which is in the Book of Revelation, to His (Christ's) "servants," wherever they may be on planet earth.

Here is the reference:

> "3 Blessed is he that readeth, and they that hear the words of this prophecy, and keep those things which are written therein: for the time is at hand." Revelation 1:3

Did you notice; the above verse says, "Blessed is he that readeth." And it also says, "Blessed" are "they that hear the words of the prophecy." And the angel says, "Blessed" are they who "keep those things which are written therein." And the reason for all of these blessings is simply because Jesus wants you to be saved into His kingdom where there is no sin but happiness and contentment. And if you understood the "prophecy" of the book of Revelation, you would not be deceived. You would know all of the humungous sequential events that will come to pass upon the citizens of the world and

The Book of Revelation an Overview

how you can escape the deceptions that will ferociously surface, how to recognize them, and how to avoid them.

Therefore, a person who is seeking understanding of "the prophecy" of the book of Revelation should not be discouraged because if you are a person who has repented and desires to abide by the statutes and commandments of Jesus Christ, the promise is and the blessings are sufficiently there for you to understand the book of Revelation. As you have noted, the reason Jesus gave "the prophecy" in the book of Revelation, in the first place, is to "1 to shew unto His servants things which must shortly come to pass." The preceding statement means what it says; Jesus Christ the LORD is going to reveal the "prophesy" of the book of Revelation to His repentant sinners ("His servants" v.1). They will know and understand the words of "the prophecy" and its symbolism.

Here is the reference:

> "1 The Revelation of Jesus Christ, which God gave unto Him, to shew unto His servants things which must shortly come to pass; and He sent and signified it by His angel unto His servant John" Revelation 1:1

As you have read in the above verse, the operative word is "shew" (show). Therefore the revelation of Jesus Christ the LORD is to show unto His servants, "things which must shortly come to pass." That is why Apostle John was told,

> "10 And he saith unto me, Seal not the sayings of the prophecy of this book: for the time is at hand." Revelation 22:10

So, to recap: "The revelation of Jesus Christ," was given to Christ's angel who, in turn, gave that revelation ("the

The testimony of Jesus Christ

testimony of Jesus Christ") to Apostle John; and Apostle John was the one,

> "2 Who bare record of the word of God, and of the testimony of Jesus Christ, and of all things that he saw." Revelation 1:2

And that record, which Apostle John wrote in a book, now we refer to it by the title of "The Revelation of St. John," which is in error because the revelation of the "prophecy" is not from Apostle John; it comes from Jesus Christ the LORD God of Israel. The title of the book should read The Revelation of Jesus Christ because Apostle John only "bare record" of "the testimony of Jesus Christ." John did not and does not reveal it. Jesus Christ reveals it. If Jesus does not want to reveal to us the meaning of "the Testimony of Jesus Christ," which is "the spirit of prophecy," we would be oblivious to the coming horrendous events that are spoken in "the prophecy." Rev. 1:3

"The testimony of Jesus" _____ In addition, in regards to the "testimony of Jesus Christ" the LORD, as you have read above (Rev. 1:2), it is revealed to Christ's "servants." And to further confirm that fact, here is the reference where the angel of the LORD tells Apostle John that his (John's) brethren "have the testimony of Jesus."

> "10 And I fell at his feet to worship him. And he said unto me, See thou [you] do it not: I am thy [your] fellowservant, and of thy [your] brethren that have the testimony of Jesus: worship God: for the testimony of Jesus is the spirit of prophecy." Revelation 19:10

Therefore, since the angel of the LORD, in the above

The testimony of Jesus Christ

verse, states unequivocally that each of John's brethren have "the testimony of Jesus Christ" the LORD, it means that they are fellow servants of the LORD who understand the "prophecy" ("testimony of Jesus Christ"), which is in the book of Revelation.

In addition, the angel of Christ the LORD goes one step further and confirms that "the testimony of Jesus" "is the spirit of prophecy." Consequently, we can also say, "the spirit of prophecy is the testimony of Jesus." For that reason, we can equate "the spirit of prophecy," of the book of Revelation, to the "the testimony of Jesus."

And since it is given to each penitent sinner to understand "the testimony of Jesus" because "the time is at hand," and since "the testimony of Jesus" is the "spirit of prophecy," it means that each penitent sinner of Jesus Christ the LORD has the "spirit of prophecy" today; they understand it, speak about it, and teach it.

In support to the above statements, we are told that the "spirit of prophecy" is understood by Apostle John's brethren, and by the "servants" of Jesus Christ. They are they who keep the Covenant (the 10 Commandments of God), as they are given to us (Acts 7:38) from Exodus 20:1-17. We are told that they each have and understand "the testimony of Jesus Christ," which "is the spirit of prophecy."

Here is the reference:

> "17 And the dragon [Satan; Revelation 12:9] was wroth with the woman [Revelation 12:2], and went to make war with the remnant of her seed, which keep the commandments of God, and have the testimony of Jesus Christ." Revelation 12:17

It should be noted from the above verse, it is the

The testimony of Jesus Christ

Commandment keepers (Exodus 20:1-17) of God who have "the testimony of Jesus," and not the Commandment breakers. The above verse says that the commandment keepers "have the testimony of Jesus Christ." They have "the testimony of Jesus" because they understand, by the power of God the Holy Spirit, about what Jesus has testified in the book of Revelation. If they did not understand "the testimony of Jesus," they would not have it, preach it, or have the ability to explain it.

Therefore, those individuals who read the book of Revelation, and those who hear the words of the book of Revelation, and those who "keep those things which are written" in the book of Revelation are "blessed" by God the Christ, by God the Father, and by God the Holy Spirit. And the reason those individuals will receive a blessing and understanding of the "prophecy" is simply because "the time is at hand" for "the prophecy" to be revealed to Christ's repentant sinners wherever they are on planet earth.

Here is the reference:

> "3 Blessed is he that readeth, and they that hear the words of this prophecy, and keep those things which are written therein: for the time is at hand." Revelation 1:3

Therefore what the book of Revelation does is to describe the final horrendous sequential evil events and acts of the unrepentant sinners who will impose their evil will by civil law, politically and religiously, upon all of the people on planet earth. And these political and religious laws, which will carry the death penalty, and not being able to buy or sell (Rev. 13:16, 17), will be imposed upon all who will not conform to do their evil will, and join them to fight Jesus Christ, indirectly, by persecuting and killing His repented followers; and that includes Apostle John and whoever else is alive with him for

The testimony of Jesus Christ

the past 2,000 years?

I hope, just about now, you are not jumping up and down in disgust or in your fury because I made the above statement that Apostle John will also be killed. Bear with me for now; I will definitely provide you with the verses so that you can read them and confirm what I have said is one hundred percent correct.

Moreover, the book of Revelation was not written to conceal "the prophecy" of the "testimony of Jesus Christ" the LORD of hosts. If it was, why was it presented to Apostle John and have him go to the lengths of writing it in the first place?

But, since "the testimony of Jesus Christ" was personally dictated to Apostle John, it reveals the importance of the prophecy, the accuracy, and the urgency of its message to the penitent sinners of Jesus Christ. It reveals the horrendous sequential events of the prophecy, which are to take place during when "the time is at hand."

For more detailed information on the sequential events of "the prophecy," read my book by the title *The Sign in Matthew 24* By: Philip Mitanidis.

Nonetheless, it should be noted, irrespective of what Satan, his evil angels, evil men, and evil women volley upon the book of Revelation and upon God's people; they will not prevail over "the prophecy" to misrepresent it or to destroy it. The book of Revelation was written to reveal "the prophecy" of the book when "the time is at hand"; and that time is the period we are living in. The fact that God's people, today, can understand "the prophecy," of the book of Revelation, confirms that we are living during the time period where "the time is at hand."

I have given you the foregoing information in order to encourage you to read the book of Revelation; and to let you know that "the testimony of Jesus Christ" is "the spirit of prophecy," which is to be revealed when "the time is at hand."

A Warning

A Warning _____ Adding to or deleting the words of the book of Revelation or deleting letters, verses, chapters, and any of the books of the Bible, as you in all probability have read before, there is a very strong condemnation upon its offenders.

And, as you most likely know, there are a number of specific warnings regarding the sixty-six books of the Bible to individuals who add and delete the word of God; or, "preach any other gospel" than that, which Jesus and the apostles have preached (Matthew 24:14). And one of those warnings, which I want to quote for you, is found in the book of Galatians. The warning is given to us by Apostle Paul; he says,

> "8 But though we, or an angel from heaven, preach any other gospel unto you than that which we have preached unto you, let him be accursed." Galatians 1:8

Very strong language don't you think?
Apostle Paul says, "let him be accursed."

Therefore, if a person from a religious body claims to have a prophet in their midst, and claim to have writings from that prophet, and those writings are contrary to what Jesus and the apostles have preached, Apostle Paul says very bluntly, "8 But though we, or an angel from heaven, preach any other gospel unto you than that which we have preached unto you, let him be accursed." Galatians 1:8

Jesus also warned in regards to people preaching another Gospel than what He preached; He made it very clear, He said,

> "14 And this gospel of the kingdom shall be

A Warning

preached in all the world for a witness unto all
nations; and then shall the end come."
Matthew 24:14

Therefore be careful not to accept another Gospel; if
you do, you will be deceived and do the devil's deviant work.
Jesus warned, if you are not with Me you are against Me.
Here is the reference:

"30 He that is not with Me is against Me; and he
that gathereth not with Me scattereth abroad."
Matthew 11:30

But, in additions to what Jesus Christ the LORD of
hosts, Apostle Paul, and the other prophets of the LORD of
hosts have stated, you will find that there is an added warning
in the book of Revelation. It says,

"18 For I testify unto every man that heareth the
words of the prophecy of this book, If any man
shall add unto these things, God shall add unto
him the plagues that are written in this book:

"19 And if any man shall take away from the
words of the book of this prophecy, God shall
take away his part out of the book of life, and
out of the holy city, and from the things which
are written in this book." Revelation 22:18, 19

As you have read, the above warning is specific as to
what would happen to an individual who adds or deletes from
what Apostle John has already written in the book of
Revelation. Therefore the book of Revelation is not to be
rewritten, altered, or tampered in any shape or form. The book

A Messenger Sent to Apostle John

of Revelation is to remain in tacked as Apostle John wrote it when he was in exile on the volcanically formed Isle of Patmos.

But, if a person chooses not to take heed to Apostles John's warning, and that person willfully adds words to the book of Revelation that person will suffer the wrath of the plagues that are spoken in "the prophecy." These plagues, which will be poured upon the unrepentant sinners, without mercy, will take place just before Jesus returns the second time to take His penitent people to heaven.

Moreover, if a person deletes words from the book of Revelation that person's name would be removed from the book of life, and access to New Jerusalem will be denied.

Needless to say, at this point, be careful what you say, preach, or write about the book of Revelation. Although retribution will not come right away, upon those who delete or add to the book of Revelation, as it did upon the children of Israel, sooner or later, according to the warning, retribution without mercy will come upon those individuals who misrepresent the words of this "prophecy."

A Messenger Sent to Apostle John _____ Christ sent His angel to Apostle John to give him a message; and that message was "Thou [you] must prophesy again." But, what was he to "prophesy again"?

The dialogue with his visitor is as follows:

> "1 And I saw another mighty angel come down from heaven, clothed with a cloud: and a rainbow was upon his head, and his face was as it were the sun, and his feet as pillars of fire" Revelation 10:1

As you have noted, Apostle John clearly states that he "saw" a "mighty angel." He states that he saw an "angel." He did not say that he saw Seraphim or Cherubim or any other

A Messenger Sent to Apostle John

type of an angel. He said, "angel."

Angels, as you probably already know, have two wings to fly with; whereas a Seraph has more than two wings to fly with (The word Seraphim is in the plural form. The word Seraphims, in the OKJV, is also in the plural form.)

Angels who are identified in the Bible with two wings are said to be messengers. They are superior to man. They are supernatural beings; and they live in the third heaven. Jesus spoke of them as a higher and different order of beings than man (Matthew 22:30; Mark 12:25). And, as messengers and protectors of repentant sinners, we have many examples in the Bible where they are seen interacting with human beings.

Here are few examples. In the Old Testament (OT), Moses describes how the "angel of the LORD" attended to the needs of Hagar the bondwoman. The angel talks with her at the well, and eventually tells her to go back to the house of Abraham. See Genesis 16:7-12.

Likewise, angels went to visit Lot, Abraham's nephew, and told him that he was in danger; and therefore he and his family had to leave Sodom quickly because Christ the LORD of hosts was going to destroy the city. See Genesis chapter nineteen.

And looking in the book of Acts, we see angels ministering to the early Christians. They opened prison doors, unshackled the victims and set them free (Acts 5:19; 12:7-11). Angels guided them in the missionary work (Acts 8:26); and inspired nonbelievers to seek the Gospel message from the apostles (Acts 10:1-7) etc. etc.

And in regards to Seraphims, here are few references, which reveal that they are different than the two winged angels.

> "1 In the year that King Uzziah died I saw also
> the LORD sitting upon a throne, high and lifted
> up and His train filled the temple.

A Messenger Sent to Apostle John

"2 Above it stood the seraphims: each one had six wings; with twain he covered his face, and with twain he covered his feet, and with twain he did fly.

"3 And one cried unto another, and said, Holy, holy, holy, is the LORD of hosts [Christ]: the whole earth is full of His glory.

"4 And the posts of the door moved at the voice of him that cried, and the house was filled with smoke.

"5 Then said I, Woe is me! for I am undone; because I am a man of unclean lips, and I dwell in the midst of a people of unclean lips: for mine eyes have seen the King [Christ: See Matthew 21:5; John 12:41.], the LORD of hosts [Christ]." Isaiah 6:1-5

According to verses two and three above, Seraphims have six wings. Isaiah states that the Seraphims used two wings to cover their faces, two wings to cover their feet, and the other two wings were used to fly. Although four of the Seraphims wings were used to cover their feet and faces, these four wings are also used for other purposes, such as hovering and agile maneuverability, as an example.

You can also read 2 Chronicles 3:14 where Solomon took the time to reconstruct very meticulously the Sanctuary in Jerusalem after the pattern, which Moses built; and if you recall, the Sanctuary, which Moses built was destroyed by the Philistines in a place called "Shiloh." (Shiloh is about 25 miles north of Jerusalem.)

Although the Philistines destroyed the Sanctuary of

A Messenger Sent to Apostle John

Christ, the Ark of the Covenant was saved and the two angels.

Nonetheless, Apostle John saw a mighty angel come down from heaven; and he noticed that the angel was "clothed with a cloud." To be "clothed" with clothes is one thing, but to be clothed with a cloud is definitely different. Therefore, was the angel "clothed with a cloud" from head to toe, or was the angel "clothed with a cloud" away from the angel's body leaving the angel's body exposed so that Apostle John was able to see the angel separately from the "cloud"? Personally, I would say the latter because Apostle John was able to discern the legs, the hands, the face, the little book in the angel's hand, the angel's head, and above the angels head a rainbow. And Apostle John was also able to tell us that the angel positioned his right foot in the sea, and his left foot he positioned on land, making the angel appear mighty and enormous.

In addition, Apostle John describes the angel's appearance as awesome, by saying to us that the angel's face was as bright as the sun; and his feet looked like two pillars of fire.

So! Is the above description of the angel literal or is it figurative?

Obviously it is literal because angels have the capability to present themselves to us in any shape, size, or form they want to. Therefore there is no shortage of the overwhelming appearance of the angel presenting himself to Apostle John in the form he describes him.

But, if you want to think of the angel's appearance in terms of being figurative, then you would have to look for Scripture where the prophet or the angel of the LORD or Jesus Christ the LORD gives you the meaning of the angel's presentation. And if you are unable to find an explanation of the angel's appearance, then logically, and Scripturally, you would have to accept the fact that the angel's appearance is literal.

A Messenger Sent to Apostle John

Simplistically put, Apostle John says,

> "1 And I saw another mighty angel come down from heaven, clothed with a cloud: and a rainbow was upon his head, and his face was as it were the sun, and his feet as pillars of fire" Revelation 10:1

> "2 And he had in his hand a little book open: and he set his right foot upon the sea, and his left foot on the earth," Revelation 10:1, 2

In addition, we are told that the angel had a "little book open" in his hand. Which hand the little book resided in is not revealed. But the little book was small enough and light enough for Apostle John to take it out of the angel's hand.

But, before Apostle John took the book out of the angel's hand, as the angel was poised with his right foot in the sea and the left foot on land, at one point, the mighty angel of the LORD,

> "3 cried with a loud voice, as when a lion roareth: and when he had cried, seven thunders uttered their voices.

> "4 And when the seven thunders had uttered their voices, I was about to write: and I heard a voice from heaven saying unto me, Seal up those things which the seven thunders uttered, and write them not." Revelation 10:3, 4

As Apostle John observed the angel, and wondered what was next, the angel roared like a lion, and when he did, Apostle John heard seven thunders. And these seven thunders

A Messenger Sent to Apostle John

A Messenger Sent to Apostle John

spoke ("uttered their voices"). And when Apostle John poised himself to write what the seven thunders said, he was told, by a "voice from heaven," to "Seal up those things which the seven thunders uttered, and write them not." Revelation 10:4

Why do you think the seven thunders were mentioned when the intent was to seal what they said?

Could it be that whatever the seven thunders uttered, they are going to be revealed later?

Who do you think will tell us what the seven thunders said?

But, as Apostle John listened intently, and looking at the angel of the LORD, he also saw one of the angel's hands rising "to heaven." And when he did, he heard the angel "sware by Him [Christ] that liveth for ever and ever, who created heaven, and the things that therein are."

Here are the references:

> "5 And the angel which I saw stand upon the sea and upon the earth lifted up his hand to heaven,

> "6 And sware by Him [Christ] that liveth for ever and ever, who created heaven, and the things that therein are, and the earth, and the things that therein are, and the sea, and the things which are therein, that there should be time no longer:" Revelation 10:5, 6

The angel in the above verses swore by Him (Jesus Christ the LORD), who created the heaven and the earth. I put in brackets the word "Christ" after the word "Him," in v.6, to let you know that it was Jesus Christ the LORD of hosts who created "all things," by Himself ("by Myself"), and "for Himself." In fact Christ says that He "maketh all things; that

A Messenger Sent to Apostle John

stretcheth forth the heavens alone."

Did you hear that?

Jesus Christ the LORD says, He created "all things," "alone," and by Himself ("by Myself"). And Apostle Paul also acknowledges that "all things" were created "by [δι'] Him" (Christ), and "for Him" Jesus Christ the LORD.

Here are the references:

> "24 Thus saith the LORD, thy [your] Redeemer, and He that formed thee [you] from the womb, I am the LORD that maketh all things; that stretcheth forth the heavens alone; that spreadeth abroad the earth by Myself" (Isaiah 44:24).

> "16 For by Him [Christ] were all things created, that are in heaven, and that are in earth, visible and invisible, whether they be thrones, or dominions, or principalities, or powers: all things were created by Him [Christ], and for Him [Christ]:" Colossians 1:16

Noticeably in the above verse (v.24), the word Christ the LORD God of Israel uses to identify and isolate Himself from God the Father and from God the Holy Spirit is "Redeemer." In fact, He says to the children of Israel that He is "thy [your] Redeemer." And in addition He also say that there is only one Redeemer.

Here is the reference:

> "11 I, [even] I, am the LORD; and beside Me there is no Saviour." Isaiah 43:11

Likewise, in the New Testament, the prophet of Jesus

A Messenger Sent to Apostle John

Christ the LORD God of Israel makes the same claim; in reference to Jesus Christ the "stone" (Acts 4:11), he says:

> "12 Neither is there salvation in any other: for there is none other name under heaven given among men, whereby we must be saved." Acts 4:12

Therefore, Christ the LORD God of Israel, who claims to be Israel's "Redeemer," is the Individual who created "all things" "16 that are in heaven, and that are in earth, visible and invisible, whether they be thrones, or dominions, or principalities, or powers: all things were created by Him [Christ], and for Him [Christ]" (Colossians 1:16). And as Christ the LORD says, "24 I am the LORD that maketh all things; that stretcheth forth the heavens alone; that spreadeth abroad the earth by Myself" (Isaiah 44:24).

In the above verses, you can readily see that there is no co-Creator involved with Jesus Christ the LORD. We are told by Apostle Paul that it was Christ who created "all things" "by Him [Christ], and for Him [Christ]" (Colossians 1:16). And Christ personally claims that He created "all things" "alone" and as He says, He created the earth "by Myself." Isaiah 44:24. In fact Apostle Paul states in the Greek text that "all things" came into existence "out of Him" (εξ αυτου), they did not come from somebody else. Here is the verse in the Greek text:

> "36 Επειδη εξ αυτου, και δι' αυτου, και εις αυτον ειναι
> Because out of Him, and by Him, and for Him are
>
> τα παντα αυτω η δοξα εις τους αιωνας. Αμην."
> the all things to Him the glory for ever. Amen
> Ρωμαιους 11:36 (Romans 11:36). (Translation is mine.)

A Messenger Sent to Apostle John

The Greek text above clearly states, "εξ αυτου" (out of Him or from Him if you like), and "δι' " (by) Him (Christ), and "εις αυτον" (for Him) are "all things."

If the "all things" came from somebody else, as some suggest, we can say that somebody created through Christ; but since Apostle Paul states unequivocally that "all things" came "out of Christ" or "from Christ" (εξ αυτου), we can agree that "all things" were created, as Apostle Paul writes, "δι' " (by) Christ.

I know many Bibles use the uninspired word "through" in Colossians 1:16 and elsewhere in the New Testament (NT); but the word "through" does not exist in the Greek text in all of the creation verses of the Bible. The Greek word is (δι'); and when it is translates into English, it will read "by."

But, all of the translators, theologians, men of the cloth, and laymen who are bent on using the uninspired word "through," to indicate that somebody was creating "through" Jesus Christ the LORD, they are not only adding sin upon themselves, for deleting words and adding uninspired words in the New Testament creation verses, at the same time, they are posturing the New Testament creation verses in contradiction to the Old Testament creation verses. In doing so, they are calling Jesus Christ the LORD God of Abraham a liar because Christ stated over and over again that He created "all things" "alone," and as He says, "by Myself." Isaiah 44:24

Therefore, since Jesus Christ the LORD God of Abraham created "all things" "alone," and by Himself ("by Myself"), God the Father or anyone else cannot claim that they are the principal creators; or claim that they created "all things" "through" Jesus Christ the LORD as many theologians and Bible translators have claimed and are claiming in their mistranslated Bibles.

What part or parts or meaning of the words "alone" and "by Myself" and "from Him" and "by Him" and "for

A Messenger Sent to Apostle John

Him" do people not understand in the creation verses of Isaiah 44:24, Romans 11:36, and Colossians 1:16?

As per Scripture, God the Father did not create anything "through" Jesus Christ the LORD God of Israel; God the Father is not the Creator of "all things." I encourage you to take the time and look at all of the creation verses in the (OT) and in the (NT), and when you do, you will notice that the uninspired word "through" does not exist in the Hebrew or in the Greek text in all of the creation verses.

Further confirmation that Jesus Christ the LORD of hosts created "all things," He said to the House of Judah,

> "4 command them [the delegates who had come to Jerusalem] to say unto their masters, Thus saith the LORD of hosts, the God of Israel; Thus shall ye [all of you] say unto your masters;

> "5 I have made the earth, the man and the beast that are upon the ground, by My great power and by My outstretched arm, and have given it unto whom it seemed meet unto Me." Jeremiah 27:4, 5

If you want more detailed information on the creation verses of the Bible and the Creator, read my book by the title *"The Creator of Genesis 1:1 Who is He?* By: Philip Mitanidis.

Moreover, the angel of the LORD swore by Christ the Creator of "all things." Apostle John writes:

> "6 And sware by Him [Christ] that liveth for ever and ever, who created heaven, and the things that therein are, and the earth, and the things that therein are, and the sea, and the things which are therein, that there should be

A Messenger Sent to Apostle John

time no longer:" Revelation 10:6

The reason the angel of Jesus Christ the LORD swore by Jesus Christ was to announce, "that there should be time no longer:" Revelation 10:6

And when should there "be time no longer"?

According to the angel of the LORD, he claims that it will take place when the seventh angel begins to sound.

Here is the reference:

> "7 But in the days of the voice of the seventh angel, when he shall begin to sound, the mystery of God should be finished, as he hath declared to His servants the prophets." Revelation 10:7

According to Revelation 11:15, the seventh angel will begin to sound, right after Revelation 11:14, when the angel of the LORD finishes his dialogue with Apostle John in the sequence of "the prophecy" (Rev. 9:20, 21 to Rev. 11:14).

Given that the second "woe" of the plagues will pass, and the third "woe" is to come (Rev. 11:14) when the angel of the LORD finishes revealing, to Apostle John, the events of chapters ten and eleven of the book of Revelation, then the third "woe" will take place. And when it does, we are told,

> "14 The second woe is past; and, behold, the third woe cometh quickly.

> "15 And the seventh angel sounded; and there were great voices in heaven, saying, The kingdoms of this world are become the kingdoms of our Lord, and of his Christ; and He [Christ] shall reign for ever and ever." Revelation 11:14, 15

A Messenger Sent to Apostle John

We are told in the above verse, when "15 the seventh angel sounded;" Apostle John could hear "great voices in heaven, saying, The kingdoms of this world are become the kingdoms of our Lord, and of his Christ." And that acknowledgement, by the multitude of heavenly voices, sets up the procedural activities in heaven to prepare the events for Jesus Christ the LORD God of Abraham to receive His creation and the creatures therein, which Christ left in God the Father's keeping (John 16:15), while Christ went on the mission to save planet earth and the penitent sinners thereof.

Here is Christ's claim:

> "15 All things that the Father hath are Mine: therefore said I, that he shall take of Mine, and shall shew it unto you." John 16:15

Jesus is clear in the above verse. He states, "all things the Father hath are Mine." Notice, Jesus does not acknowledge that "all things" are or belong to God the Father or to anybody else. Jesus says unequivocally that "all things...are Mine." And Jesus adds that God the Father will "take" of what is Christ's "and shall shew it unto you [the apostles]."

There is no confusion in the above verse; Jesus states plainly, "All things that the Father hath are Mine." And "shall take of Mine, and shall shew it unto you."

In addition to the above claims, here are few references, where we are told where God the Father will give back to Jesus Christ, "all things," which Jesus Christ the LORD of hosts created. Apostle Paul writes, "24 Then cometh the end, when he shall have delivered up the kingdom to God [Christ], even the Father; when he shall have put down all rule and all authority and power. 25 For he must reign, till he hath put all enemies under His feet." 1 Corinthians 15:24, 25

Preferably, you read the above two verses in the Greek

text; but if you can't, here is a clarification of the verses by adding the information in brackets. The verses will read as follows:

> "24 Then cometh the end, when he [God the Father] shall have delivered up the kingdom to God [God the Christ], even the Father; when he [God the Father] shall have put down all rule and all authority and power.

> "25 For he [God the Father] must reign, till he [God the Father] hath put all enemies under His feet [Christ's feet: Psalm 110:1]." 1 Corinthians 15:24, 25 (See also Hebrews 1:8.)

Thus, according to the above two verses, the "end" will come, "when he [God the Father] shall have delivered up the kingdom to God [God the Christ]." In addition, we are told, "even the Father; when he [God the Father] shall have put down all rule and all authority and power."

Then Apostle Paul makes an unexpected statement, he says,

> "25 For he [God the Father] must reign, till he [God the Father] hath put all enemies under His feet [Christ's feet: Psalm 110:1]." 1 Corinthians 15:25

According to the above verse, God the Father is going to reign over "all things" until such time he puts Christ's enemies under Christ's feet. And after God the Father submits "all things" to Christ, under His feet [See Psalms 110:1; Hebrews 1:8.], and he stops reigning, Christ the LORD of hosts begins to "reign for ever and ever" over "all things."

Here is the reference:

A Messenger Sent to Apostle John

> "15 And the seventh angel sounded; and there
> were great voices in heaven, saying, The
> kingdoms of this world are become the
> kingdoms of our Lord, and of his Christ; and
> He [Christ] shall reign for ever and ever."
> Revelation 11:15

As per the above verse (v.25), when God the Father stops reigning ("must reign, till he [God the Father] hath put all enemies under His [Christ's] feet," and Christ begins to reign "for ever and ever" (v.15), what is God the Father going to do with himself?

Picture it?

After God the Father gives back or submits everything ("all things"), to Jesus Christ, what is God the Father going to do; he appears oh so alone and isolated?

Although the above two verses (1 Corinthians 15:24 and 25) appear to isolate God the Father from Christ and Christ's universe, Apostle Paul does explain the outcome in 1 Corinthians 15:28.

Apostle Paul writes:

> "28 And when all things shall be subdued unto
> Him, then shall the Son also himself be subject
> unto him that put all things under Him, that
> God may be all in all." 1 Corinthians 15:28

Unfortunately, there is a problem with the above verse; it is mistranslated.

According to the mistranslated verses, God the Father is subjected to God the Christ (v.24) and God the Christ is subject to God the Father (v.28). And yet, God the Holy Spirit is not subject to anyone? And, even man is not subject to anyone; as per Scripture, he is a free moral agent!

A Messenger Sent to Apostle John

Man as a free moral agent can subject himself to Christ and be saved for eternity; or man can subject to Satan, to idols, or to no one, if he can; and at the end, he will die in his sins.

Nonetheless, verse twenty-eight, like many other mistranslated verses, misleads a person to believe that Jesus Christ with His creation is to be subjected to God the Father, after God the Father subjects Christ's enemies under Christ's feet.

I do not know of a single verse in the entire Hebrew and Greek text where it plainly states Jesus Christ the LORD subjects to God the Father. If you find such a verse, I would more than welcome your e-mail.

If a person is to accept the above mistranslated verse, a person would believe that Christ is going to receive "all things," which Christ created, from God the Father. And, when Christ receives "all things," which He created, from God the Father, Christ then begins to reign over "all things."

Consequently, we can ask, how long is Jesus Christ going to reign over His creation?

According to Revelation 11:15, Christ reigns "for ever and ever" over His creation ("all things").

But, if Christ subjects to God the Father, how is Christ going to reign over "all things" "for ever and ever"?

And when Christ re-subjects the "all thing" back to God the Father, does that mean God the Father, starts to reign again and Christ does not?

If so, why is Scripture saying, Christ is going to "reign for ever and ever."

And, over what is God the Father going to reign, given that Christ would already be reigning over "all things"?

Moreover, since "all things" that the Father has are Christ's, why are they returned to Christ in the first place, if Christ is only going to give them back to God the Father? And why does the mistranslated verse claim only Jesus Christ is

A Messenger Sent to Apostle John

going to be subjected to God the Father and not God the Holy Spirit?

How does the above make any sense to you?

Although the verses in 1 Corinthians 15:24 and 25 explain the transition taking place between God the Father and God the Christ, the mistranslated verse (v.28) in the English rendering contradicts vs. 24 and 25.

The verse in its mistranslated form states,

> "28 And when all things shall be subdued unto Him [Christ], then shall the Son also himself be subject unto him that put all things under Him [Christ], that God may be all in all." 1 Corinthians 15:28

Noticeably, in the above, mistranslated verse, the words "also himself" do not exist in the Greek text; but what does exist right after the word "Son" (Υιος) is the word "θελει" (wants, desires). Therefore, the verse will read reasonably close to the Greek text, as follows: "then He the Son wants [or desires if you like] to subject to the subjector, to him the all things, so that God [God the Christ, God the Father, God the Holy Spirit] may be in all." 1 Corinthians 15:28

Consequently, if you read v.28 without the uninspired added words ("also himself"), you will observe that the verse clearly states that whatever God the Father subjects ("all things" – not Christ) to Christ that is what Christ subjects back to God the Father. Christ does not subject Himself to God the Father because according to the Greek text, Christ is not subjected to God the Father or any one else.

Let me say again, according to the Greek text, Jesus Christ is not subjecting Himself to God the Father; neither is God the Father subjecting himself to Christ, even though the mistranslated verse implies that God the Father is subject to the

A Messenger Sent to Apostle John

Son by the use of the words "even the Father" (v.24) is "delivered" to Christ.

It should also be noted, Christ's "all things," which He created, are already subjected, by Jesus Christ, to God the Father; and they will be subjected up until God the Father puts all of Christ's enemies under Christ's feet (Psalms 110:1; Hebrews 1:8). Then, God the Father subjects the "all things" to Christ. And when he does, he stops reigning (v.25). And then Christ begins to reign; and when he does, Christ re-subjects the "all thing," which He has created back to God the Father so that "God may be in all."

Let me reiterate, what Apostle Paul is simply saying to us in the Greek Text (v.28) is the fact that Jesus Christ the LORD God of His universe and of all that is in it and outside of it is going to receive His Kingdom, which Christ left in God the Father's keeping; and when He does, Christ will choose to share "all things" with God the Father so "that God [God the Christ, God the Father, and God the Holy Spirit] may be all in all." 1 Corinthians 15:28

You know, we can continue with the above dialogue and write twenty or more pages, but the bottom line is to consider the verses in 1 Corinthians 15:24, 25, and 28 in the Greek text, and also seriously consider Christ's following statement, which reveals that Christ is not subjected to anyone and neither will He be in the future.

> "6 Jesus saith unto him, I am the way, the truth, and the life: no man cometh unto the Father, but by Me." John 14:6

Did you notice? Christ the LORD says, "no man cometh unto the Father, but by Me." There is exclusion in that statement. You cannot bypass Jesus Christ and go directly to God the Father. You cannot exclude Jesus Christ. Neither can

A Messenger Sent to Apostle John

God the Father exclude Jesus Christ because without Jesus Christ, God the Father cannot save you or anyone else from eternal ruin. Christ must be put first, then God the Father. Does that sound to you that Christ is subjected or He is going to be subjected to God the Father?

Obviously not!

But, by His wisdom, what is going to be subjected by the free will of Jesus Christ the LORD of hosts, to God the Father, are the "all things" Jesus has created, and that includes all of the redeemed from planet earth, so that "God (God the Christ, God the Father and God the Holy Spirit) may be "all in all." 1 Corinthians 15:28

For God the Christ, and God the Father, and God the Holy Spirit to "be all in all," "all things" must be subjected to Them, so that They "all" can be "in all."

Simplistically, it should be noted, if Jesus Christ the LORD God of hosts does not subject the "all things," to God the Father and to God the Holy Spirit, God the Father and God the Holy Spirit would be excluded from the "all things," which Jesus Christ the LORD has created. But as free moral agents Jesus welcomes Them to reign with Him in unity of purpose over "the all things," which Christ has created.

That template can readily be observed in the book of Revelation chapter four.

If you are going to read Revelation chapter four, read it in the Greek text because the translators have mistranslated this chapter in four major points.

Nonetheless, after the voice from heaven told Apostle John not to write what the seven thunders uttered; the voice from heaven instructed him to go and take the little book from the angel's hand.

"8 And the voice which I heard from heaven
spake unto me again, and said, Go and take the

A Messenger Sent to Apostle John

little book which is open in the hand of the angel which standeth upon the sea and upon the earth." Revelation 10:8

Obedient to the voice from heaven, Apostle John said,

"9 And I went unto the angel, and said unto him, Give me the little book. And he said unto me, Take it," Revelation 10:9

But, after Apostle John went to the angel, who stood in the sea and on land with his feet, the angel reached out and gave the little book to Apostle John; and when he gave it to him, he said;

"9 Take it, and eat it up; and it shall make thy [your] belly bitter, but it shall be in thy [your] mouth sweet as honey." Revelation 10:9

A Messenger Sent to Apostle John

Although Apostle John did not know how hard it was going to be to eat the little book; nonetheless, he patiently obeyed the angel's command and ate it. And when he did, he did notice that it was sweet as honey in his mouth; but, when the little book reached Apostle John's belly, it was predominately bitter.

Apostle John wrote,

> "10 And I took the little book out of the angel's hand, and ate it up; and it was in my mouth sweet as honey: and as soon as I had eaten it, my belly was bitter." Revelation 10:10

What kind of material the little book was made from is not revealed? How many pages the little book contained are also not disclosed? What message or messages the little book contained are also not revealed to us.

And, we can ask, will the messages of "the seven thunders" and of "the little book" be revealed to us when Apostle John comes out in the open to "prophesy again" before nation, people, kindred, and tongues?

Time will tell.

ILILILILILILIL

You Must Prophesy Again

*You must
  prophesy again*

One thing is for sure, after Apostle John ate the little book, he was told by the angel of the LORD of hosts that he "must prophecy again."

Here is the angel's command:

"11 And he [the angel] said unto me [Apostle John], Thou [you] must prophesy again before many peoples, and nations, and tongues, and kings." Revelation 10:11

"You must prophecy again"!
What a thing to say to Apostle John!
Really?
Why "must" he "prophesy again"?
And, when "must" he "prophesy again"?
A very direct command was given by the angel of Christ the LORD to Apostle John. The angel said, "you must prophesy again before many peoples, and nations, and tongues, and kings." The angel's command was made very specific and personal by the use of the pronoun "you." Although the angel does not reveal to us what Apostle John was to prophecy again,

You Must Prophecy Again

he did reveal that his prophecy would cover a very large territory by saying, "you must prophesy again before many peoples, and nations, and tongues, and kings."

In passing, let me make an important point. The fact that we can come to the point of understanding "the testimony of Jesus Christ," reveals that we are living in the time where the prophet says, "the time is at hand."

So! Why am I sticking my neck out under such severe warning; and state Apostle John is going to personally prophecy again, when everybody else believes Apostle John died between 98-117 AD, and is not with us?

Actually I am not sticking my neck out on a limb. I am simply stating a Scriptural fact that Apostle John is still alive today on planet earth; and he is patiently waiting to "prophesy again" during the time of the fulfillment of "the prophecy," which is taking place right now. And, in confirmation to that fact, noticeably, we find the conversation between Christ's holy angel and Apostle John taking place between the end of "the second woe" of the plagues (Revelation 9:21), and the beginning of the "third woe" of the plagues (Revelation 11:15). And that conversation between Apostle John and Christ's holy angel can be found in chapters ten and eleven of the book of Revelation.

Although we are not told what Apostle John is to prophecy again; we can consider the possibilities and conclude, it could very well be the utterance of the "seven thunders," or the content of "the little book," which Apostle John did eat, or the prophecy could very will be something new, and appropriate to the time period Apostle John is to "prophesy" "before many peoples, and nations, and tongues, and kings"?

In any case, one thing is for sure, the angel of the LORD did say to Apostle John,

Is Apostle John Still Alive Today *By: Philip Mitanidis*............97

"11 Thou [you] must prophesy again before

You Must Prophecy Again

many peoples, and nations, and tongues, and kings." Revelation 10:11

So far, for the past 2,000 years, there have been no hyped historical events heralded throughout the world, which depicts Apostle John preaching to the masses of the world covertly. Neither has it been said, at any time in the past 2,000 years that Apostle John has been known to be appearing publicly, identifying himself, and prophesying "before many peoples, and nations, and tongues, and kings"?

And yet, the angel of Christ the LORD of hosts said to Apostle John;

"Thou [you] must prophesy again."

So! When is Apostle John going to "prophesy again"?

Obviously, as per Scripture, Apostle John is to "prophesy again" during the time when the "prophecy" of the book of Revelation is being fulfilled right before our eyes. And the fact that the beginning of the "prophecy" is being fulfilled today, and Apostle John is to "prophesy" during the fulfillment of "the prophecy" that means that the revelation to the world, by this book that Apostle John is still alive today is a forerunner to his appearance in his 2,000 years old body.

And when he does reveal himself to the world, oh, what gripping stories he would be able to tell.

But, I am sure, none that Satan, his evil angels, and his satanic agencies would like the people of planet earth to hear.

REVELATION TEN (OKJV)

"1 And I saw another mighty angel come down from heaven, clothed with a cloud: and a rainbow was upon his head, and his face was as it were the sun, and his feet as pillars of fire. 2 And he had in his hand a little book open: and he set his right foot upon the sea, and his left foot on the earth, 3 And cried with a loud voice, as when a lion roareth: and when he had cried, seven thunders uttered their voices. 4 And when the seven thunders had uttered their voices, I was about to write: and I heard a voice from heaven saying unto me, Seal up those things which the seven thunders uttered, and write them not.

"5 And the angel which I saw stand upon the sea and upon the earth lifted up his hand to heaven, 6 And sware by him that liveth for ever and ever, who created heaven, and the things that therein are, and the earth, and the things that therein are, and the sea, and the things which are therein, that there should be time no longer: 7 But in the days of the voice of the seventh angel, when he shall begin to sound, the mystery of God should be finished, as he hath declared to his servants the prophets.

"8 And the voice which I heard from heaven spake unto me again, and said, Go and take the little book which is open in the hand of the angel which standeth upon the sea and upon the earth. 9 And I went unto the angel, and said unto him, Give me the little book. And he said unto me, Take it, and eat it up; and it shall make thy belly bitter, but it shall be in thy mouth sweet as honey. 10 And I took the little book out of the angel's hand, and ate it up; and it was in my mouth sweet as honey: and as soon as I had eaten it, my belly was bitter.

"11 And he said unto me, Thou must prophesy again before many peoples, and nations, and tongues, and kings."
Revelation 10:1-11

gg

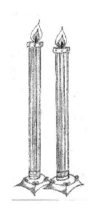

THE TWO
WITNESSES

The two witnesses, who are they, what are they witnessing, and to whom are they going to witness?

Previously, if you recall, the angel of the LORD of hosts said to Apostle John,

"Thou [you] must prophecy again."

The angel of the LORD of hosts, who was standing with his right foot in the sea and with the other foot on land, gave Apostle John a "reed" that looked like a "rod." Although the "rod" is not described whether it was flexible or not, and how long it was, and what kind of measuring tool it represented, the angel told Apostle John to go and measure with the "rod" that was given to him, the Temple of God, the altar, and them that worship therein.

Apostle John said,

"1 And there was given me a reed like unto a rod: and the angel stood, saying, Rise, and measure the temple of God, and the altar, and them that worship therein." Revelation 11:1

The measurements of the Temple ....
Although the angel of Christ the LORD of hosts told Apostle John to measure the Temple, the altar, and the worshippers that are inside the

The Measurements of the Temple

Temple, there is no input given to us, in this chapter, regarding the measurements of the Temple, altar, and of the worshippers "therein"?

But because the Temple had worshippers "therein," we can conclude that these worshippers are not worshipers in the padlocked restricted ruined Sanctuary, which exists on earth, in the city of Jerusalem. According to 1 Kings 9:1-9, Christ the LORD of hosts, who appeared to Solomon the second time (1 Kings 9:2), said to King Solomon that He would dwell in Zion in the "most holy place" of the Sanctuary. But, if the children of Israel choose to serve other gods, the Sanctuary in Jerusalem would be in ruins and it will remain in ruins.

Here are the references:

> "7 Then will I cut off Israel out of the land which I have given them; and this house, which I have hallowed for My name, will I cast out of My sight; and Israel shall be a proverb and a byword among all people:

> "8 And at this house, which is high, every one that passeth by it shall be astonished, and shall hiss; and they shall say, Why hath the LORD done thus unto this land, and to this house?

> "9 And they shall answer, Because they forsook the LORD their God, who brought forth their fathers out of the land of Egypt, and have taken hold upon other gods, and have worshipped them, and served them: therefore hath the LORD brought upon them all this evil." 1 Kings 9:7-9

As a result, since the Sanctuary in Jerusalem is under

The Measurements of the Temple

lock and key today, we can conclude, there are no worshippers with their sin offerings, or thank offerings, in the eastern part of the courtyard of the Sanctuary, waiting to appear before Christ the LORD of hosts who use to reside in the "most holy place" of the Sanctuary above the "mercy seat."

Since there are no worshippers in the earthly Temple with their burnt offerings, we can conclude that the Temple Apostle John was asked to measure was the heavenly Temple.

Although we are not given the measurements of the heavenly Sanctuary in this chapter, we can see the resemblance by the earthly Sanctuary. And the reason we can see the similarities is due to the fact that Christ the LORD of hosts told Moses, while the children of Israel were staying at the foot of Mt. Sinai, to make the earthly Sanctuary in the same pattern as the heavenly Sanctuary.

To give you an idea how large the earthly Sanctuary was, as per the pattern that was provided to Moses by Christ the LORD of hosts, while they were on top of Mount Sinai, we can use the Mesopotamian measurement of a cubit, which equals to 19.6 inches in length. Or, we can use the Egyptian measurement of a cubit, which equals to 20.6 inches length. Here are the measurements of the earthly Sanctuary, which Moses built.

The tabernacle, the dwelling place of Christ the LORD of hosts, was contained in an area of 30 cubits in length, by 10 cubits in width, and 10 cubits in height. The 30 cubits in length faced south and the 10 cubits faced east. The tabernacle had two compartments. The first compartment, which had a door facing east, was 10 cubits wide by 20 cubits long; and it was identified by the name of "the holy place."

"The holy place" contained the "alter of incense" (Exodus 30:1-10), the "table of showbread" (Exodus 25:23-30), "lampstand" (Exodus 25:31-40), "veil" (Exodus 26:31), which divided the two rooms, and allowed the Levi priest to enter

The Measurements of the Temple

from "the holy place" into the "most holy place" of the tabernacle, once a year. And it had a door made out of linen curtains that was facing eastward.

The second compartment's dimensions were 10 cubits by 10 cubits, and it was identified by the name of "the most holy place." It contained "the Ark of the Covenant" (chest), which was made from acacia wood. It had two poles extending from either side of the chest, which were used to carry the chest. The poles remained un-removed from the golden rings of the chest. The chest was overlaid with gold inside and out. It had on top of the chest, on each end, a cherub (Exodus 25:18) facing downward in the chest. And each cherub had one of their wings extended upward touching each other's wings (Exodus 37:8, 9). And in between the two cherubs, on top of the chest, there was a block of solid gold, which was identified as the "mercy seat" (Exodus 25:17). The "mercy seat" was where Christ the LORD of hosts inhabited. And there the Shekinah glory of Christ the LORD could be seen. The "mercy seat" was also used to give access to the storage area, inside the chest, where the Ten Commandments on two tablets of stone stood. The dimensions of the Ark of the Covenant are as follows: 2 ½ cubits long, 1½ cubits wide, and 1 ½ cubits high (Exodus 25:10). In addition, in the "most holy place," there were the writings of the ceremonial law leaning on the side of the Ark of the Covenant, and Aaron's staff, which budded, was in the room.

Although the earthly Temple with the Ark of the Covenant pails in comparison to the heavenly temple, at least it gives us a since of understanding of what is the heavenly Temple's purpose and what it looks like.

Here is the reference where it reveals the Ark of the Covenant exposed in heaven in the Temple of God:

"19 And the temple of God was opened in

heaven, and there was seen in his temple the ark of His testament: and there were lightnings, and voices, and thunderings, and an earthquake, and great hail." Revelation 11:19

Furthermore, the tabernacle, which contained the two rooms, was surrounded by a fence, which was 50 cubits wide, 100 cubits long, and 5 cubits high. The fence was made by using 10 (50/5) by 20 (100/5) pillars spaced 5 cubits apart, and linen curtains 5 cubits high by 5 cubits wide covered each pillar, which in turn enclosed the courtyard (Exodus 27:18). And on the east side of the courtyard's fence, there was a door made of linen curtains, which allowed the penitent sinner access into the courtyard of the Sanctuary, in order to offer a sin offering or a thank offering to Christ the LORD of hosts, on the altar of sacrificial burnt offerings, which was located near the door of the eastern courtyard's fence, and in between the tabernacle.

Thus, the earthly Sanctuary consisted of a tabernacle with dimensions of 30 cubits long by 10 cubits wide by ten cubits high; and it was enclosed by a fence 50 cubits wide by 100 cubits long and by 5 cubits high.

The Altar of Incense _____ Apostle John was also

The Altar of Incense

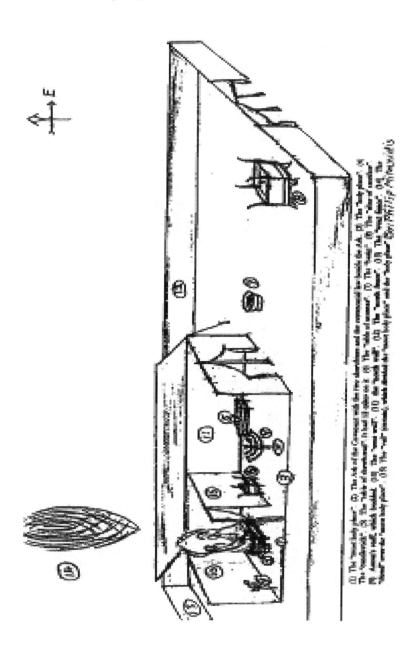

Measuring the Worshippers

asked to measure "the altar of incense," which was placed in the west side of the room of "the holy place." It was placed near the veil, which separated the two rooms (The veil, in the earthly Sanctuary, rent in two from top to bottom when Christ died on the cross Matthew 27:51; signifying that the ceremonial law was terminated. Ephesians 2:14, 15.).

The "altar of incense" (Exodus 30:1-10) had on top of it four horns, one horn on each corner. It was where the Levi priest touched the blood of the animal from the sin offering for the penitent sinner. And it was where the Levi priest stood before "the altar of incense" and offered the daily prayers before Christ the LORD of hosts who dwelt on the other side of the veil, in the "most holy place," above the "mercy seat" of the Ark of the Covenant.

The measurements of "the altar of incense," are as follows: one cubit square by two cubits high. The "altar of incense was also overlaid with pure gold.

I hope the above brief presentation gave you a good overview of the earthly Sanctuary, and therefore a glimpse of the heavenly Sanctuary.

Measuring the Worshippers .... The other request of the angel of the LORD of hosts to Apostle John was to go and measure the "worshippers" that were "within" the Temple.

Did you notice? The angel of the LORD of hosts said, "worshippers." They are not mediators.

So! What are worshippers doing inside the heavenly Temple?

Consider the following. In the earthly Temple (tabernacle), which Moses and King Solomon had built separately, Jesus Christ the LORD God of Israel dwelt in "the most holy place," above "the mercy seat," and in between the two Cherubims, of the Ark of the Covenant. And from there, Jesus Christ the LORD judged His people; and by His grace

Measuring the Worshippers

By Philip Mitanidis

covered the penitent sinner's sins. The penitent sinner's sins were covered until such time Jesus Christ paid for their sins by dying on Calvary's cross. And when Jesus was resurrected, all of the penitent sinners, who had died in Christ the LORD God of Abraham, starting with Able, the first martyr, and right up until the Cross, their sins that were covered were completely removed from those penitent sinners. In doing so, today, in their dusty and watery deathbeds, they all remain holy before Christ the LORD of hosts waiting for His return.

If Jesus Christ the LORD God of His universe did not sacrifice Himself on Calvary's cross 2,000 years ago, your sins, my sins, and all who have lived and died, they all would have died as sinners. Likewise, all sinners who are dying today, they too would be dying as sinners. And therefore, there would be no hope for salvation and eternal life. Eventually, planet earth, Satan, Satan's evil angels, men, women, and all life forms would progressively disintegrate because of their sins, and be no more; unless Jesus Christ the Creator of "all things," in His mercy stops all suffering by eliminating planet earth before it disintegrates.

But, since Jesus Christ sacrificed Himself on Calvary's

Measuring the Worshippers

cross for the penitent sinners, now we are living under Christ's grace. Therefore there is hope for the penitent sinner who wants to live in a sinless universe with other sinless created beings. And, as history has indicated, there are a lot of people who, since the fall of Adam and Eve, have chosen Jesus Christ as their LORD, God, and Savior. In doing so, they also have chosen eternal life where there is righteousness, happiness, and contentment throughout eternity in Christ's Kingdom.

Today, we are saved by Christ's grace and not by works. You don't have to bring a lamb to sacrifice for your sins in the eastern courtyard of the sanctuary in Jerusalem. Jesus Christ the LORD is the sacrificial Lamb who taketh away our sins (John 1:29).

Therefore, today, just like before the cross, there are people who want to live in righteousness and be saved in Christ's Kingdom. And, according to "the prophecy" of the book of Revelation, there will be a multitude of people who would be saved during the "great tribulation" (Revelation 13:11-18), which has already started.

And in reference to "the prophecy" and how many people are going to be saved, we are told of their number and that number according to "the prophecy," is innumerable.

Here is the reference:

> "9 After this I beheld, and, lo, a great multitude, which no man could number, of all nations, and kindreds, and people, and tongues, stood before the throne, and before the Lamb, clothed with white robes, and palms in their hands;" Revelation 7:9

So! Who is this "great multitude, which no man could number"?

According to verse fourteen, of Revelation seven, they

are penitent sinners who came out of "the great tribulation."
Here are the references:

> "13 And one of the elders answered, saying unto
> me, What are these which are arrayed in white
> robes? and whence came they?

> "14 And I said unto him, Sir, thou [you]
> knowest. And he said to me, These are they
> which came out of great tribulation [Matthew
> 24:21], and have washed their robes, and made
> them white in the blood of the Lamb."
> Revelation 7:13, 14

As you have read in the above verses, the innumerable "multitude" that comes out of "the great tribulation," as per "the prophecy" of the book of Revelation, is to be fulfilled during the coming political and religious events implemented by civil law, by Britain and USA, which they have already started. (We are living in the time period of events that are depicted in the twelfth verse of Revelation chapter thirteen.) If you want more detailed information, read my book called, *The Sign in Matthew 24* By: Philip Mitanidis.

Therefore during that time period of the "great tribulation," "the prophecy" (Revelation 13:11-18), which will be rapidly fulfilled, there will be horrific atrocities done throughout the world to nonconformists and to God's people; therefore their prayers will be ascending to the heavenly Temple quite frequently, and be received by Jesus Christ their "Mediator"

Here is the reference:

> "5 For there is one God, and one Mediator
> between God and men, the man Christ Jesus;"

Measuring the Worshippers

1 Timothy 2:5 (See also Galatians 3:20.)

But, "immediately" after the "great tribulation," and after "the sign" of Jesus Christ second coming appears in heaven, for the entire world to see, who is going to be left in the heavenly Temple?

As per the angel of the LORD of hosts, it's the "worshippers." But who are the "worshippers"?

a). We can conclude, the "worshippers" are the penitent people who came out of "the great tribulation," and others after the "great tribulation" who might want to be saved. And we can also conclude that they are the ones the angel of the LORD wanted Apostle John to "measure" or count if you like?

So! How does Apostle John "measure" or calculate the number of "worshippers" that are in the heavily Temple?

Obviously in this case he cannot because the answer is already given. We are told that the worshippers are a "great multitude which no man could number."

Here is the reference:

"9 After this I beheld, and, lo, a great multitude, which no man could number, of all nations, and kindreds, and people, and tongues, stood before the throne, and before the Lamb, clothed with white robes, and palms in their hands" (Revelation 7:9).

Therefore, we could conclude that the "worshippers" are,

"14 they which came out of great tribulation [Matthew 24:21; Revelation 13:11-18], and have washed their robes, and made them white in the blood of the Lamb.

Measuring the Worshippers

> "15 Therefore are they before the throne of
> God, and serve Him day and night in His
> temple: and he that sitteth on the throne shall
> dwell among them." Revelation 7:14, 15

Although Apostle John was given the privilege to see in
"the prophecy" of the book of Revelation, what happens to
Christ's penitent sinners that are going to be persecuted, and
many of them killed, during "the great tribulation"; it must
have been quite a relief to Apostle John to hear that in spite of
the horrendous evil the political and religious authorities are
going to inflict upon Christ's penitent people, and upon the
nonconformists, during the "great tribulation" and onward,
there would be innumerable penitent sinners saved. And as
Apostle John wrote, there would be "a great multitude [saved],
which no man could number, of all nations, and kindred, and
people, and tongues."

Here is the reference:

> "9 After this I beheld, and, lo, a great multitude,
> which no man could number, of all nations, and
> kindreds, and people, and tongues, stood before
> the throne, and before the Lamb, clothed with
> white robes, and palms in their hands"
> (Revelation 7:9).

The "great multitude" that survives the relentless
persecution and comes through the "great tribulation" is
depicted in the above verse as a saved "multitude." And this
saved "multitude" that comes through "the great tribulation,"
many of the "multitude" will continue to live in their sinless
state on earth. They will continue to live on earth with others
until Jesus comes the second time to take His penitent people
to the third heaven to appear before Him while He is sitting on

Measuring the Worshippers

His throne.

But, before a great multitude appear before the throne of Christ the LORD, these individuals from the "multitude" would still be living on earth with others who choose to repent, while the plagues of Revelation chapters eight and nine continue to fall one after another upon the unrepentant sinners and upon the ecosystem of the earth. And while the redeemed live on earth amongst the evil rampant chaos, and utter destruction, their prayers would continue to be received, by God the Holy Spirit, and carried to Jesus Christ our "Mediator," in the heavenly Temple (Romans 8:26).

Therefore, the penitent "worshippers," the angel of the LORD wanted Apostle John to count in the Temple, are identified as a "great multitude" who came out of the "great tribulation," living on earth while the plagues continue to fall on the unsaved wicked, and upon the ecosystem of the earth. And during those devastating times, the great multitude's prayers will ascend to Jesus Christ in the heavenly Temple. And since the prayers of the "great multitude" are in the heavenly Temple, we could conclude, they are "the worshippers," the angel of the LORD wanted Apostle John to measure (calculate).

b).   Although it is a foregone conclusion that the prayers of the saints are taken by God the Holy Spirit to Jesus Christ, their Mediator, with "groanings," which they could not utter (Romans 8:26); we can also conclude that the "worshippers" the angel of the LORD wanted Apostle John to count were the angels that are worshiping in the Temple.

If you recall, although Jesus Christ the LORD of hosts was in the "most holy place" of the earthly tabernacle, there were worshippers who officiated in the tabernacle. In this case it was the Levi priests who worshipped before "the table of incense" or "altar" if you like. And the Levi priests also

The Court

worshipped before Christ the LORD of hosts in the "most holy place" once a year, even thought Moses frequently worshipped there.

That being the case, we can count in the heavenly Temple, with Apostle John those worshippers—at least the angels that are revealed to us after the "third woe," when the seventh angel sounds (Revelation 11:15). And when the seventh angel sounds that will bring us to chapters fourteen and fifteen. And when we go to those two chapters, we can count the number of angelic worshippers there are in the Temple of God. In Chapter fourteen there are three angels (Revelation 14:15, 17, 18) revealed that are worshipping in the Temple. And when we look in chapter fifteen, we see seven angels (Revelation 15:1, 6) worshipping in the temple. And when we add up the angels from the two chapters that are worshipping in the Temple, we get a total of ten angelic worshippers.

On the other hand, we can go one step further and conclude that the angel of the LORD of hosts wanted Apostle John to measure or count all of the worshipers in the Temple of God; and that would include the saints and the angels. And when we do, we get a number, which says, no man could number.

The Court _____ But, in consideration of the court, which is outside of the Temple, Apostle John was told not to measure it. And the reason the angel of the LORD of hosts gave Apostle John was because it was given to the Gentiles. The word Gentile is commonly referred to as an unbeliever of the Bible, to pagan believers, and is commonly viewed in contrast to a Jew before Jesus was crucified and to a Christian after Jesus was crucified.

But, in regards to the "court," here is what the angel said to Apostle John:

The Court

> "2 But the court which is without the temple
> leave out, and measure it not; for it is given
> unto the Gentiles: and the holy city shall they
> tread under foot forty and two months."
> Revelation 11:2

As you read above, the court is given to the Gentiles
(unbelievers). And the reason it is given to the Gentiles is due
to the fact that they refuse to repent and accept Jesus Christ as
their LORD God and Savior. Therefore there is no "Mediator"
in the heavenly Temple of God to accept them or their prayers.
They and their prayers are left outside of the Temple of God to
perish. And because of their abomination, sin drenched bodies
and minds, and hatred towards Jesus Christ, and His penitent
sinners, they and their prayers would not be carried by God the
Holy Spirit, from earth, and into the heavenly Temple for Jesus
Christ the LORD of hosts to consider.

BY: PHILIP MITANIDIS

Here are the references, which give us a glimpse of the
wicked, their character, and of their un-repented attitude, which
takes place at the end of "the second woe" of the plagues:

> "20 And the rest of the men which were not

The Court

> killed by these plagues [Revelation chapters. 8 &
> 9] yet repented not of the works of their hands,
> that they should not worship devils, and idols of
> gold, and silver, and brass, and stone, and of
> wood: which neither can see, nor hear, nor
> walk:

> "21 Neither repented they of their murders, nor
> of their sorceries, nor of their fornication, nor
> of their thefts." Revelation 9:20, 21

A very defiant portrayal of the abomination of the un-
repented wicked hearts of men and women, who continue to
persecute God's people, refuse to repent from their evil works,
and continue to worship devils, idols, and "Neither repented
they of their murders, nor of their sorceries, nor of their
fornication, nor of their thefts" (v.21). Therefore let me say
again; they and their repulsive prayers are not taken into the
heavenly Temple by God the Holy Spirit because God the Holy
Spirit does not make "intercession" for the wicked un-
repentant people. They are left outside of the Temple in their
sinful perverted unnatural state. And in that evil wicked state,
we are told that "the holy city [Jerusalem] shall they tread under
foot."

How long are these unrepentant evil sinners going to
"tread under foot" the holy city?

The angel of the LORD said, "forty and two months."

And how long are forty and two months?

As per the Bible calculations, a month has thirty days
and a year has twelve months. Therefore if we divide forty-two
months by twelve months per year it will equal to $42/12 = 3.5$
years. Consequently, the Gentiles (unbelievers) are going to
"tread" Jerusalem for forty-two months, just before the city is
going to be devastated with a great earthquake, which would

Empowering the Two Witnesses to "prophesy"

cause seven thousand people to die in the ruins.

Empowering the Two Witnesses to "prophesy" _____ After the angel of the LORD of hosts finished his dialogue with Apostle John about "the Temple," "the altar of incense," "the worshippers," and "the court," he said to Apostle John,

> "3 And I will give power unto my two witnesses, and they shall prophesy a thousand two hundred and threescore days, clothed in sackcloth." Revelation 11:3

As per the above verse, the angel of the LORD mentioned three important points to Apostle John in regards to the "two witnesses" of Revelation chapter eleven.
They are:

1). Give power unto my two witnesses.
2). Prophesy for 1,260 days
3). Dressed in sackcloth

1). As per the above verse (v.3), what kind of power is given to the "two witnesses" that are identified as,

> "4 These are the two olive trees, and the two candlesticks standing before the God of the earth." Revelation 11:4

Noticeably, the "two olive trees, and the two candlesticks" in v.4 are also identified in v.3 as the "two witnesses," and visa versa. And in Revelation 11:10, the "two witnesses" are further identified as the "two prophets" of the LORD of hosts who receive power
What kind of power are the "two witnesses" given?

Empowering the Two Witnesses to "prophesy"

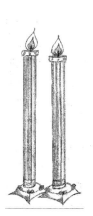

Obviously, the "two witnesses" are given power that goes beyond their own capability, in order for them to accomplish their mission. And that power is God the Holy Spirit. Without God the Holy Spirit's guidance and support in their ministry, testimony, and in their "prophecy," the "two witnesses" would not be able to accomplish their mission. In fact it would be a failed mission. I state that it would be a failed mission because the "two witnesses" do not know what is in the hearts of the un-repentant sinners? Are the sinners seeking salvation, or are they plotting to kill the "two witnesses." Therefore the "two witnesses" would be limited in their outreach with their messages and to protect themselves. But, with the power of God the Holy Spirit, their protection and capabilities to reach the hearts of men and women would be limitless.

Here is an example of the power of the Holy Spirit.

If you recall, after Christ's resurrection, the apostles were to meet with one accord in their faith in the upper room in the city of Jerusalem. And when they did, they all received the power of God the Holy Spirit.

Apostle Luke writes:

"1 And when the day of Pentecost was fully come, they were all with one accord in one place. 2 And suddenly there came a sound from heaven as of a rushing mighty

Empowering the Two Witnesses to "prophesy"

wind, and it filled all the house where they were sitting.

"3 And there appeared unto them cloven tongues like as of fire, and it sat upon each of them.

"4 And they were all filled with the Holy Ghost, and began to speak with other tongues, as the Spirit gave them utterance.

"5 And there were dwelling at Jerusalem Jews, devout men, out of every nation under heaven. 6 Now when this was noised abroad, the multitude came together, and were confounded, because that every man heard them speak in his own language.

"7 And they were all amazed and marvelled, saying one to another, Behold, are not all these which speak Galilaeans? 8 And how hear we every man in our own tongue, wherein we were born?

"9 Parthians, and Medes, and Elamites, and the dwellers in Mesopotamia, and in Judaea, and Cappadocia, in Pontus, and Asia, 10 Phrygia, and Pamphylia, in Egypt, and in the parts of Libya about Cyrene, and strangers of Rome, Jews and proselytes, 11 Cretes and Arabians, we do hear them speak in our tongues the wonderful works of God.

"12 And they were all amazed, and were in doubt, saying one to another, What meaneth this?

Then Apostle Peter said, "36 Therefore let all the house of Israel know assuredly, that God hath made that same Jesus, whom ye have crucified, both LORD and Christ.

Empowering the Two Witnesses to "prophesy"

"37 Now when they heard this, they were pricked in their heart, and said unto Peter and to the rest of the apostles, Men and brethren, what shall we do?

"38 Then Peter said unto them, Repent, and be baptized every one of you in the name of Jesus Christ for the remission of sins, and ye shall receive the gift of the Holy Ghost. 39 For the promise is unto you, and to your children, and to all that are afar off, even as many as the Lord our God shall call. 40 And with many other words did he testify and exhort, saying, Save yourselves from this untoward generation.

"41 Then they that gladly received his word were baptized: and the same day there were added unto them about three thousand souls. 42 And they continued stedfastly in the apostles' doctrine and fellowship, and in breaking of bread, and in prayers.

"43 And fear came upon every soul: and many wonders and signs were done by the apostles. 44 And all that believed were together, and had all things common; 45 And sold their possessions and goods, and parted them to all men, as every man had need. 46 And they, continuing daily with one accord in the temple, and breaking bread from house to house, did eat their meat with gladness and singleness of heart, 47 Praising God, and having favour with all the people. And the Lord added to the church daily such as should be saved." Acts 2:1-12, 36-47

Therefore, God's people, wherever they are on planet earth, like the apostles of old, they are to propagate the Gospel of Jesus Christ the LORD of hosts throughout the world by

Empowering the Two Witnesses to "prophesy"

the power of God the Holy Spirit in order to reach the sinner's hearts.

But, sometimes power is also given to His penitent people by Christ's Spirit.

The prophet of Christ the LORD of hosts said,

> "6 Then he answered and spake unto me, saying,
> This is the word of the LORD unto
> Zerubbabel, saying, Not by might, nor by
> power, but by My spirit, saith the LORD of
> hosts." Zechariah 4:6

Likewise, the "two witnesses," who already have received power by God the Holy Spirit, can also receive power from Christ the LORD of hosts at any given point to help them succeed with their assignment; especially when they testify and prophesy for three and a half years (Rev. 11:3) in Jerusalem before kindred, tongue, kingdoms, and nations.

It must be remembered, the "two witnesses" are going to find themselves in a very hostile environment when they publicly reveal themselves before the masses in Jerusalem. They would not only need power from on high, but also protection because the un-repentant sinners are going to be aggravated and "tormented" (Rev. 11:10) when they hear what the "two witnesses" say to them; for that reason, the wicked are going to try their utmost to kill them (Rev. 11:5, 6, 7).

Therefore the "two witnesses" are going to need all the power they can get from God the Holy Spirit in order to accomplish their 2,000-year-old mission.

But because the "two witnesses" are going to find themselves in a very hostile territory for three and a half years in Jerusalem, the "two witnesses" are given instant protection from their wicked enemies.

Apostle John writes:

Empowering the Two Witnesses to "prophesy"

"5 And if any man will hurt them [the "two witnesses"], fire proceedeth out of their mouth, and devoureth their enemies: and if any man will hurt them, he must in this manner be killed." Revelation 11:5

When you read throughout the Bible the enormous ways the wicked have killed the prophets of the LORD of hosts, — even Jesus Christ the Creator of "all things" — you will notice that the prophets of the LORD of hosts did not retaliate upon their evil abusers; and when they did, it was not always an instant retaliation. But, in the case of the "two witnesses," retribution will come instantaneously upon those who try to do them harm.

Apostle John writes "if any man will hurts them," (the "two witnesses"), they are instantly protected and can simply speak and fire will come upon those individuals who are trying to do them harm. As soon as the words are uttered by the "two witnesses" retribution falls upon their adversary. As an example, if the wicked try to beat the "two witnesses" brutally, the "two witnesses" can stop the mob by commanding fire to fall upon them and devour them. If the wicked try to run over the "two witnesses with a vehicle, the "two witnesses" can command fire to fall upon those individuals that are in the vehicle; and consequently, not only the wicked individuals in the vehicle will burn to death, but also the vehicle will catch fire and therefore explode into flames. If a mob was to club the "two witnesses" into a coma, the "two witnesses could bring fire upon the mob and devour them; or they could allow the mob to go instantly into coma, or allow the mob to taste the pain and suffering from their clubs before the wicked strike the "two witnesses"; or the wicked can suffer prolonged pain, which they were going to inflict upon Apostle John and his associate.

Empowering the Two Witnesses to "prophesy"

In addition, as per the above verse, if the wicked try to kill the "two witnesses" of the LORD of hosts ("the two prophets of the LORD of hosts Revelation 11:10), the prophet of the LORD states that those who are trying to kill the "two witnesses," "must in this manner be killed."

Therefore, if a person or persons try to kill the "two witnesses," those individuals are going to be killed instantaneously in the same manner they were trying to kill the "two witnesses." Consequently, if a person tries to kill the "two witnesses" with a sword, the killer would automatically be killed in the same way he was trying to kill the "two witnesses." If a sniper was hired to kill the "two witnesses" with a long-range rifle, the sniper would be killed with the very same bullets he was trying to kill the "two witnesses." If the wicked men and women try to lynch the "two witnesses," the wicked would be hung in the same manner they were going to string up the "two witnesses." If the wicked try to drown the "two witnesses," the wicked would drown in the same way they were going to drown the "two witnesses." If the evil men and women try to blow up the "two witnesses," the wicked would be blown to bits in the same manner they were going to blow up the "two witnesses."

Since the "two witnesses" cannot be killed or hurt by their enemies, the wicked would be frustrated and furious and aggravated and tormented to no end; and therefore wanting, oh so desperately to depose, sent them away, or even kill them in order to silence them.

Furthermore, in the days of the "two witnesses," as they "prophesy," the "two witnesses" have power to stop the heaven from raining, to make water undrinkable, and to smite the earth with as many plagues they want and as often they want and wherever they want.

The prophet of the LORD of hosts writes:

"6 These [the "two witnesses"] have power to

shut heaven, that it rain not in the days of their prophecy: and have power over waters to turn them to blood, and to smite the earth with all plagues, as often as they will." Revelation 11:5

According to the above verse, during the days of their "prophecy" [the 3.5 years of prophecy in Jerusalem], the "two witnesses" have the power to stop the clouds from raining during those three and a half years of their "prophecy." Or they can make the rain to stop raining as often as they want and as long as they want and wherever they want. The "two witnesses can also smite the water and make it undrinkable for as long as they want and wherever they want. Likewise the "two witnesses" can smite the earth with all manner of plagues, as frequently as they want and wherever they want the plagues to strike.

Consequently because the wicked men and women of the world are going to be grieved and "tormented" by the acts and words of the "two witnesses," the wicked will try all manner of ways to kill the "two witnesses" even though they know that they cannot kill them. The wicked have heard and have the above testimony (Revelation 11:3-6), which plainly states that no human being will be able to kill the "two witnesses." But, in their defiant evil attitude, they still think that they can; and to their detriment, they will keep trying unsuccessfully.

As you have read in verses five and six, the "two witnesses" are the ones that are given awesome powers to protect themselves during their 3.5 years of "prophecy." If any wicked human being or human beings who are trying to kill them or do them harm, the "two witnesses can command

"5 fire proceedeth out of their mouth, and devoureth their enemies: and if any man will

Empowering the Two Witnesses to "prophesy"

hurt them, he must in this manner be killed."
Revelation 11:5

Noticeably, since this "prophecy" (of the book of Revelation) was given 2,000 years ago and the "two witnesses" have been standing before "the God of the earth," I can say, although evil men and women from all walks of life for the past 2,000 years have not being able to kill the "two witnesses," the most daring efforts will be attempted by the wicked upon the "two witnesses," during their 3.5 years of "prophecy" in Jerusalem. And after the "two witnesses" finish their "testimony," Satan will be able to make war with the "two witnesses," and eventually, prevail over them, and killed them.
Here is the reference:

"7 And when they [the "two witnesses"] shall have finished their testimony, the beast that ascendeth out of the bottomless pit shall make war against them, and shall overcome them, and kill them." Revelation 11:7

As per the above verse, we are told that the "two witnesses" will accomplish their mission at the end of their three and a half years of "testimony" in Jerusalem, "before many peoples, and nations, and tongues, and kings" (Revelation 11:7; 10:11). And when the "two witnesses" finish their "testimony," at the end of the three and a half years, "the beast" from the "bottomless pit" will came up and start a war with the "two witnesses." And when the battle begins to rage between the "two witnesses" and the "beast" from the "bottomless pit," the on lookers will scurry with their, cell phones, news media, videos, pictures, and all manner of electronic gadgetry trying their utmost to capture the moment of the battle. Eventually, the "beast" from the "bottomless pit" overcomes the "two witnesses" and kills them.

And when the "beast" kills the "two witnesses," the crowds become more and more ecstatic with joy. And in their joyous hype, the wicked throughout the world celebrate the kill by sending gifts to each other. And in their perverted hype and ecstasy, they will leave the dead bodies of the "two witnesses" on the street of Jerusalem where they were killed to rot, and to exhibit the kill in pride, throughout the world, as proof of their demise.

The prophet of the LORD of hosts says,

"10 And they that dwell upon the earth shall rejoice over them, and make merry, and shall send gifts one to another; because these two prophets tormented them that dwelt on the earth." Revelation 11:10

"8 And their dead bodies shall lie in the street of the great city, which spiritually is called Sodom and Egypt, where also our LORD was crucified.

"9 And they of the people and kindreds and tongues and nations shall see their dead bodies three days and an half, and shall not suffer their dead bodies to be put in graves." Revelation 11:8, 9

Although the wicked prefer to flaunt their kill as much as they can before the world masses, Christ the LORD of hosts has other plans for His "two witnesses." The dead bodies of the "two witnesses" shall not remain in Jerusalem to be turned into spectacles, or be allowed to remain on the street to decompose to oblivion. After three and a half days, the bodies of the "two witnesses" are resurrected by Jesus Christ the

Empowering the Two Witnesses to "prophesy"

LORD. And when the wicked see the "two witnesses" standing up and walking around, their arrogant hype is quickly curtailed. Instead, "great fear fell upon them which saw them."

Here are the references:

> "11 And after three days and an half the Spirit of life from God entered into them, and they stood upon their feet; and great fear fell upon them which saw them." Revelation 11:11

Great fear will fall upon the wicked indeed!

The wicked will began to wonder if it was retribution time for killing the "two witnesses." But all they had to do is to remember the words of the "prophecy" that retribution was not at hand by the "two witnesses." Retribution is coming by the hand of the angels who are ready to execute the will of the LORD.

Regrettably, the majority, if not all of the wicked of the world, after three and a half years of "testimony" by the "two witnesses," the wicked still reject the last call to repentance. At that time, since they do not want to be saved, Christ the LORD of hosts will take the "two witnesses" to heaven.

The prophet of the LORD says that the wicked (Satan, his evil angels, men, women, and children of age), at that time will hear a voice from heaven calling the "two witnesses" to come up into heaven.

Here is the reference:

> "12 And they heard a great voice from heaven saying unto them, Come up hither And they ascended up to heaven in a cloud; and their enemies beheld them." Revelation 11:12

After the wicked see the "two witnesses" gradually

disappear into heaven, they will assume everything is going to go back to what they call normal, which is their abominable evil acts, and their evil delight (2 Thessalonians 2:12). But, within the same hour the "two witnesses" were taken to heaven, there will be a great earthquake in Jerusalem, which will kill seven thousand people.

Apostle John writes:

> "13 And the same hour was there a great earthquake, and the tenth part of the city fell, and in the earthquake were slain of men seven thousand: and the remnant were affrighted, and gave glory to the God of heaven." Revelation 11:13

Finally, the wicked will acknowledge the God of heaven, and will give glory to His name. Although that acknowledgement and that glory to God is expressed after the earthquake, it is short lived because the wicked go back to their evil ways and blaspheme the God of heaven.

And, after the earthquake when the "third woe" begins, probation will close for the human race; every human being on planet earth will make a choice to accept Jesus Christ as their LORD, God, and Savior, or to reject Jesus Christ as their LORD, God, and Savior.

And at that point in time of the "prophecy," since no more people want to be saved the "third woe" is going to sound, which will usher in Christ coming in His kingdom.

The prophet of the LORD writes:

> "14 The second woe is past; and, behold, the third woe cometh quickly." Revelation 11:14

That means that the events of the "third woe" are the

Empowering the Two Witnesses to "prophesy"

preparation of Christ the LORD of hosts coming in His kingdom (v.17).

> "15 And the seventh angel sounded; and there were great voices in heaven, saying, The kingdoms of this world are become the kingdoms of our Lord, and of his Christ; and He shall reign for ever and ever.

> "16 And the four and twenty elders, which sat before God on their seats, fell upon their faces, and worshipped God,

> "17 Saying, We give thee thanks, O LORD God Almighty, which art, and wast, and art to come; because thou [You] hast taken to thee [You] thy [Your] great power, and hast reigned." Revelation 11:15-17

After Jesus takes His "great power," there is the preparation of giving the rewards (v.18) "unto thy [Your] servants the prophets, and to the saints, and them that fear thy [Your] name, small and great; and shouldest destroy them which destroy the earth."

> "18 And the nations were angry, and thy [Your] wrath is come, and the time of the dead, that they should be judged, and that thou [You] shouldest give reward unto thy [Your] servants the prophets, and to the saints, and them that fear thy [Your] name, small and great; and shouldest destroy them which destroy the earth." Revelation 11:18

In addition, there is the preparation of giving to the seven angels the last seven plagues to pour upon the ecosystem

The "Two Witnesses" personified

and upon the un-repentant men and women and of children who discern right from wrong, before Jesus Christ the LORD of hosts comes to planet earth to take His people to heaven.

Jesus Christ encourages and says, "1 Let not your heart be troubled: ye believe in God, believe also in Me. 2 In my Father's house are many mansions: if it were not so, I would have told you. I go to prepare a place for you. 3 And if I go and prepare a place for you, I will come again, and receive you unto Myself; that where I am, there ye may be also." John 14:1-3

As you have read in the above presentation, the two witnesses receive power to not only protect themselves from their enemies, but to also be capable of finishing their 3.5 years mission in Jerusalem.

The "two witnesses" personified _____ As per the above overall pages, since the "two olive trees" and the "two candlesticks," are identified as the "two witnesses," and the "two witnesses" are identified as the "two prophets" of the LORD of hosts (Rev. 11:10), we can accept the fact that the "two olive trees" and the "two candlesticks" are said to be personified in verses three to twelve. They speak, they have feelings, they retaliate, they breathe, they have human bodies, they are killed, the breath of life is taken away from them by Christ, and after three and a half days, the breath of life is put in them again by Christ, they are resurrected, and in the end, they are taken from the earth to heaven.

Therefore, the fact that these "two witnesses" (prophets of the LORD Revelation 11:10) are upon the earth, dressed in "sackcloth" clothing, and witness in Jerusalem for three and a half years, get killed, resurrected, and then taken to heaven, is a strong argument that "the two olive trees and the two candlesticks" are personified. They are human beings who stand on earth before Jesus Christ the LORD to do His will.

The fact that these "two witnesses" are alive and stand

Duration of "prophecy" + *"clothed in sackcloth"*

before Christ the LORD God of Abraham, ever since the inception of this "prophecy" (in the book of Revelation) 2,000 years ago, and continue to stand before the LORD of hosts up until the "third woe" (Revelation 11:14), and think for themselves; they give a strong indication that they have been alive ever since their birth. And since they continually stand before Jesus Christ the LORD of hosts, and tarry in His will, these two human beings must be very special unto Christ the LORD of hosts.

2). *Duration of "prophecy"* _____ And, as per Revelation chapter eleven and verse three, for how long are the "two witnesses" from Chapter eleven going to "prophesy"?

As per the angel's statement, "they shall prophesy a thousand two hundred and threescore days." And when we calculate the angel's revelation of days, we end up with the following: "a thousand two hundred and threescore days" (1,000 + 200 + 60) will equal to 1,260 days. And when we convert the 1,260 days to months they will equal to 1,260/30 = 42 months. And when we convert the months to years we will get 42/12 = 3.5 years.

Thus, as per the above calculations, the "two witnesses" are going to "prophesy" for 3.5 years.

Where are the "two witnesses" going to "prophesy"?

As per the above presentation, the "two witnesses" (the two prophets of the LORD of hosts Revelation 11:10) will "prophesy" and "testify" before all of the people in Jerusalem, for three and a half years before they are killed by the "beast" who comes out from "the bottomless pit."

3). *"clothed in sackcloth"* _____ Furthermore, we are also told in Revelation 11:3 that the "two witnesses" (prophets of the LORD, Rev. 11:10) will be "clothed in sackcloth." Sackcloth was usually very coarse and scratchy. The

"clothed in sackcloth"

cloth or garment was normally dark and woven out of goat's hair or camel's hair or both. And when the garment was worn, it symbolized, for the individual who was wearing it, a very deep heavy sorrow and mourning.

Therefore, the fact that "the two witnesses" will be wearing sackcloth garments when they reveal themselves in Jerusalem, it tells us that they would be in mourning probably for the ruined lives, which Satan, his evil angels, evil men, and evil women have done, to planet earth's ecosystem, to each other, to God's people, and for the refusal to give up their evil ways.

Here are the references:

"20 And the rest of the men which were not killed by these plagues [Revelation chapters. 8 & 9] yet repented not of the works of their hands, that they should not worship devils, and idols of gold, and silver, and brass, and stone, and of wood: which neither can see, nor hear, nor walk:

"21 Neither repented they of their murders, nor of their sorceries, nor of their fornication, nor of their thefts." Revelation 9:20, 21

Therefore, seeing that this 3.5 years event in Jerusalem is the last call to repentance to a perishing world, the "two witnesses," are going to testify to the rebellious people, in the city of Jerusalem, for three and a half years dressed in "sackcloth." And during that time they will "prophesy again before many peoples, and nations, and tongues, and kings," as a testimony to their callous, wicked, and unrepentant hearts.

"3 And I will give power unto my two witnesses,

"clothed in sackcloth"

> and they shall prophesy a thousand two hundred and threescore days [3.5 years], clothed in sackcloth." Revelation 11:3

And, during the 3.5 years of testimony by "the two witnesses," noticeably, the un-repentant sinners (Gentiles) at that same period will tread Jerusalem for three and a half years; more than likely caused by the influx of people traveling to and from to Jerusalem, trampling everything that is nonconforming to the worship of "the beast whose number is 666" (pope); and in their twisted blood thirsty rage, to hopefully see "the two witnesses" get killed or to see them performing one of their rebukes by fire, blood, or plagues.

How evil and twisted are un-repentant evil men and women going to be at that period of time and onwards?

According to Jesus Christ's words, they are going to be drenched in sin as far as their imagination will take them.

Jesus said,

> "37 But as the days of Noe [Noah] were, so shall also the coming of the Son of man be.

> "38 For as in the days that were before the flood they were eating and drinking, marrying and giving in marriage, until the day that Noe entered into the ark,

> "39 And knew not until the flood came, and took them all away; so shall also the coming of the Son of man be." Matthew 24:37-39

> "5 And GOD saw that the wickedness of man was great in the earth, and that every imagination of the thoughts of his heart was

Who Stands Before the God of the Earth?

only evil continually." Genesis 6:5

Did you notice? Jesus said that the "imagination of the thoughts of his heart was only evil continually" (v.5).

What a horrible state of mind to be in?

Can you imagine a person continually tormenting himself with the help of Satan's evil angels and craving to do evil as far as his "imagination of the thoughts of his heart" will take him to do "only evil continually"?

Did you notice the little word "only"?

That's right, Jesus said, "every imagination of the thoughts of his heart was only evil continually." What a gruesome perverted evil conditions Jesus paints of the un-repented human race during the 3.5 years of "prophesy" in Jerusalem by "the two witnesses." The thoughts of the wicked, at that time, are going to be "only evil continually."

Can you imagine the condition and the "only evil continually" mindset of the entire wicked human race? And yet, while that is going to be the condition of the world, Jesus Christ the LORD, in His mercy, is going to send "the two witnesses" for 3.5 years to Jerusalem, dressed in sackcloth to give the whole world the last call to repentance for three and a half years.

No wonder Christ the LORD has to protect the "two witnesses," otherwise the wicked will kill them as soon as they appear in Jerusalem dressed in sackcloth, and reveal to the people who they are.

Who stands before the God of the earth and who is the God of the earth? _____ According to the initial presentation by the angel of the LORD, "the two witnesses" are identified as "the two olive trees, and the two candlesticks," and visa versa.

The angels of the LORD said,

Who is "the God of the Earth"?

> "3 And I will give power unto my two witnesses, and they shall prophesy a thousand two hundred and threescore days, clothed in sackcloth." Revelation 11:3

> "4 These are the two olive trees, and the two candlesticks standing before the God of the earth." Revelation 11:4

And, as per verse four, these "two olive trees, and the two candlesticks" ("the two witnesses," v.3), "stand before the God of the earth."

So, who is "the God of the earth"?

According to Jesus Christ the LORD of hosts and the prophets of the Old Testament and by the prophets of the New Testament, Jesus Christ the God of Abraham is the God of the earth. (If you want more detailed information, read my book called *The Creator of Genesis 1:1 Who is He?* By: Philip Mitanidis.)

Christ the LORD of hosts said to the leaders of Israel,

> "4 And command them [the delegates who came to Jerusalem] to say unto their masters, Thus saith the LORD of hosts, the God of Israel; Thus shall ye [all of you] say unto your masters;

> "5 I have made the earth, the man and the beast that are upon the ground, by My great power and by My outstretched arm, and have given it unto whom it seemed meet unto Me." Jeremiah 27:4, 5

And, in the New Testament, as per the Greek text, we have the same acknowledgement in a number of references.

Who is "the God of the Earth"?

The prophet of Christ the LORD of hosts said,

"3 All things were made by Him [Christ]; and
without Him [Christ] was not any thing made
that was made.

"10 He [Christ] was in the world, and the world
was made by Him [Christ], and the world knew
Him [Christ] not." John 1:3, 10

Did you hear what Apostle John said in the above
verses?

Apostle John said, "all things were made by Him
[Christ] (v.3)."

Although the words "all things" means everything, and
that includes planet earth, Apostle John still singles out planet
earth and says, "and the world was made by Him [Christ]"
(v.10). In addition, Apostle Paul confirms that Christ is the
God of this world by stating a simple fact that "all things" were
made "by Him [Christ] and "for Him [Christ] (Colossians
1:16)."

"16 For by Him [Christ] were all things created,
that are in heaven, and that are in earth, visible
and invisible, whether they be thrones, or
dominions, or principalities, or powers: all
things were created by Him [Christ], and for
Him [Christ]:" Colossians 1:16

Since Jesus Christ created "all things" by Himself, and
for Himself, "alone," and as Christ says, "by Myself"
(Colossians 1:16; Isaiah 44:24), it means that Christ the LORD
of hosts is the God of this world because "the all things" were
not created for someone else; He created them for Himself.

Therefore "the two olive trees and the two

What Prophets are Still Alive Today?

candlesticks" ("the two witnesses") stand before God the Christ of the earth.

Let me expand on the God of the earth. Christ is the God of the earth; in fact, Christ is the God of "all things," which He created; and that includes the universe, what is inside the universe, and what is outside of the universe. In fact King Solomon sums the above quite adequately; he said,

> "27 But will God indeed dwell on the earth? behold, the heaven and heaven of heavens cannot contain thee [You]; how much less this house that I have builded?" 1 Kings 8:27

Everything evolves under Christ's administration. Therefore, "the two witnesses," who are on earth, they stand before Christ the God of the earth, giving the impression that these "two witnesses" always stand before Christ the LORD of hosts.

What Prophets are Still Alive Today? _____ Previously, we noted that the "two olive trees" and the "two candlesticks" were personified (Revelation 11:3-12). Since "the two olive trees" and the "two candlesticks" are personified to "two witnesses," and the "two witnesses" are personified to "two prophets" (Rev. 11:10) of the LORD of hosts, we can ask, who are these "two prophets" that are still alive and standing before Christ the LORD of hosts and doing His will for the past 2,000 years?

According to a handful of verses, at least one of the witnesses, who has been anointed with olive oil, like his associate, and is fortified with the light of the Gospel of Jesus Christ the LORD of hosts (Mark 1:1; Romans 1:16; Galatians 3:8), is Apostle John.

Here is why?

What Prophets are Still Alive Today?

After Jesus Christ the LORD of hosts was resurrected, before Jesus went to heaven to mediate for the penitent sinners (1 Timothy 2:5), He had a conversation with Apostle Peter. And during that conversation, in regards to Apostle John, Apostle Peter said to Jesus Christ the LORD "what shall this man do?"

Here are the references:

"21 Peter seeing him [Apostle John] saith to Jesus, LORD, and what shall this man do?

"22 Jesus saith unto him, If I will that he tarry till I come, what is that to thee [you]? follow thou [you] Me." John 21:21, 22

As per the above verses, the answer Jesus gave to Apostle Peter was simple; He said to him, why are you concerned if Apostle John remains on earth and tarries till I come?

Apostle Peter, obviously accepted Christ's statement; because after that, all of the Apostles believed that Apostle John "should not die."

Here is the reference:

"23 Then went this saying abroad among the brethren, that that disciple [Apostle John of v.22] should not die: yet Jesus said not unto him, He shall not die; but, If I will that he tarry till I come, what is that to thee?" John 21:23

Although the apostles believed, as the above verse indicates that Apostle John would not die of old age or any time soon, they understood that he would stand before Christ the LORD and "tarry until" he sees Jesus "coming in His

What Prophets are Still Alive Today?

kingdom."

Although the above verses should suffice that today Apostle John is alive and standing on earth before Christ the LORD of hosts; and that he is not going to die "till" he sees Jesus coming "in His kingdom" ("If I will that he tarry till I come"), the above verses are not the only indicators to reveal that Apostle John was not going to die any time soon, but live on until he sees Jesus coming "in His kingdom."

If you recall, the angel of Christ the LORD of hosts said to Apostle John,

> "11 Thou [you] must prophesy again before many peoples, and nations, and tongues, and kings." Revelation 10:11

The angel of the LORD did not mix his words softly to Apostle John; he said to him,

> "11 Thou [you] must prophesy again." Revelation 10:11

That was not a request. In fact, the angel said to Apostle John, "thou [you] must."

That is very precise and strong command directed to Apostle John.

In order for Apostle John to personally "prophesy again," logically and Scripturally, Apostle John had to "prophesy again" during his lifetime. But, since the life expectancy on average is around seventy-five years, we should look for evidence in Apostle John's seventy-five years of life span, and see if he had prophesied again after he wrote the book of Revelation? And if he has not, we must look beyond the seventy-five years and see if Apostle John has prophesied again "before many peoples, and nations, and tongues, and

What Prophets are Still Alive Today?

kings."

But since historically, Apostle John has not yet prophesied openly to the public again, "before many peoples, and nations, and tongues, and kings," we must look for him beyond today; and observe in the coming days when and where Apostle John is going to surface and claim, before the world that he is Apostle John. And when he does, are people going to listen to his message or messages? And will he be able to bear witness under coercion and life threatening attempts? Or, will he torment the wicked to no end by witnessing to the masses, in the name of Jesus Christ the LORD of hosts.

And since Apostle John has not witnessed up until now, and has not aggravated all of the wicked of the world, is further evidence that Apostle John has not personally "prophesied again." And that fact alone tells us that Apostle John's personal witnessing, in Jerusalem, is still in the future.

And to further confirm that the pending events of the "prophecy" by Apostle John are still in the future, here are three simple prophetic facts you can follow. First, the inhumane events of "the great tribulation," which we are living in has to rapidly be fulfilled (Revelation 13:11-18). And secondly, "immediately" after "the great tribulation," "the sign" of Christ appears in heaven for all of the people of the world to see (Matthew 24:29, 30). And three, nether chapters 8 & 9 of Revelation have taken place. These three prophetic events have not come to pass. Therefore, the final pending events of the "prophecy" by Apostle John are still in the future.

(For more detailed information on "the sign" read my book: *The Sign in Matthew 24* By: Philip Mitanidis).

But, Apostle John was not the only one to witness and prophesy for Christ the LORD of hosts.
Here is why?
Did you notice?

What Prophets are Still Alive Today?

In Revelation chapter ten and verse eleven, the angel of the LORD said to Apostle John, "thou [you] must prophesy again." But, in Revelation 11:3, the angel of the LORD said, "they shall prophesy."

Here is the reference:

"3 And I will give power unto my two witnesses, and they shall prophesy." Revelation 11:3

As per the above verse there is going to be more than one person involved in the "prophecy" by the use of the word "they" ("they shall prophesy").

And to further confirm the fact that there is going to be more than Apostle John who stands on earth before Christ the LORD of hosts, and is not going to "taste of death," "till" he sees Christ coming "in His kingdom," according to Christ's own words, noticeably there is more than one person that will "tarry till" Jesus comes "in His kingdom."

Jesus said,

"28 Verily I say unto you, There be some standing here, which shall not taste of death, till they see the Son of man coming in His kingdom." Matthew 16:28

Jesus Christ the LORD speaking to His apostles was very clear in His above statement; He said, "There be some standing here, which shall not taste of death, till they see the Son [Christ] of man coming in His kingdom."

Did you notice, in Matthew 16:28, Jesus is using the words "some standing here" to convey to His audience that there would be more than one person, who was standing there that would not die; or as Jesus stated, some people who were standing there with Him "shall not taste of death."

What Prophets are Still Alive Today?

Therefore it is evident from the above verse, since all of the apostles were with Jesus when He made the statement that "some" standing there with Him would not "taste of death," it means that Apostle John was there and the other individuals or individual was there also who would not "taste of death" "till they see the Son of man coming in His kingdom."

Therefore, we can be sure that there is going to be at least two people who are going to remain alive until they see Christ's "coming in His kingdom," and one of those individuals is Apostle John.

And in regards to Apostle Peter, according to Jesus, Apostle Peter is not one of those individuals that will not see death and tarry till Jesus comes "in His kingdom."

Here are Christ's words to Apostle Peter,

> "18 Verily, verily, I say unto thee, When thou [you] wast young, thou girdedst thyself, and walkedst whither thou wouldest: but when thou [you] shalt be old, thou shalt stretch forth thy [your] hands, and another shall gird thee, and carry thee whither thou [you] wouldest not." John 21:18

As per the above verse, Apostle Peter was going to die of old age. He was told, "when thou [you] shalt be old, thou shalt stretch forth thy [your] hands, and another shall gird thee, and carry thee whither thou [you] wouldest not." John 21:18

Therefore, who is the other person or persons that are standing before the "the God of the earth"? I am not sure?

But, this much we do know, if you recall, while Jesus Christ the LORD was on earth with His disciples, Jesus admonished His disciples whenever they were to go out on errands, on chores, or go out to witness for Him, they were to go in pairs (Mark 6:7). For that reason, and for the fact that Jesus said, "some standing here shall not taste of death," there will be at least two apostles who stand before Christ "the God of the earth" and will remain alive to accomplish their mission until Jesus comes "in His kingdom."

      Who are the "two witnesses" of Revelation chapter eleven? _____
_____ Previously, although we briefly traced in the first chapter of this book the customs and the traditional reports of all of the twelve apostle's deaths, Scripturally, there was no accountability of the deaths of ten out of twelve apostles. It was observed, Scripturally there were two apostles dead out of twelve; and we also know that at least two apostles shall not "taste of death" "till" they see Jesus coming "in His kingdom." And that makes at least four apostles accountable – plus Apostle Peter, if you like?

      But, in reference to the rest of the apostles, surprisingly Jesus said, "some" who were standing there with Him would not "taste of death" (Matthew 16:28). And after Christ's resurrection, Jesus said to Peter, "If I will that he [Apostle John] tarry till I come, what is that to thee [you]?" (John 21:22). Consequently, the above two comments strongly attest that there is going to be more than one individual, besides Apostle John that will "tarry" and "shall not taste of death, till they see the Son of man coming in His kingdom." Matthew 16:28

      And, since there is going to be at least one more person besides Apostle John that is going to remain alive and "tarry till" Jesus comes "in His kingdom," we can conclude that these two apostles have been traveling together for the past 2,000 years throughout the world spreading the Gospel message and its doctrine. And these two apostles of Christ "shall not taste of death, till they see the Son [Christ] of man coming in His kingdom." Matthew 16:28

      I stated that Apostle John and his associate are traveling throughout the world, and spreading the Gospel message for the past 2,000 years is due to the fact that these two men are

Who are the "Two Witnesses" of Rev. 11

not inactive sitting in a coffee shop all day long engaged in idle words, or walking around in a mall with nothing better to do but gossip in vain words, or gone fishing all day, or staring out the window and vegetating. All you have to do is to look at various historical pockets of communities, throughout the world for the past 2,000 years, which have received the Gospel doctrine and were persecuted for their belief in the Gospel doctrine, to show you that somebody was quite active in spreading the Gospel of Jesus Christ (Mark 1:1), in those areas.

But, Apostle John and his associate were not only to spread the Gospel and its doctrine wherever they went throughout the world, they were also told specifically to "testify" and "prophesy" openly before "kindred," "tongues," "kings," and "nations." The angel of the LORD said to Apostle John, "Thou [you] must prophesy again" (Revelation 10:11).

But, when was Apostle John going to "prophesy again" openly before "kindred," "tongues," "kings," and "nations"?

As per Scripture, consider the following:

At this point, in order to identify the "two witnesses" of Revelation chapter eleven, I am going to compare what Jesus said to His apostles, while He was on earth, with what the angel of the LORD of hosts said in the book of Revelation chapter eleven.

Here are the comparative results:

Christ's predictions	Revelation 11 predictions
"28 Verily I say unto you, There be some standing here, which shall not taste of death, till they see the Son of man coming in His kingdom." Matthew 16:28	"3 And I will give power unto my two witnesses, and they shall prophesy a thousand two hundred and threescore days, clothed in sackcloth. 4 These are the two olive trees, and the two candlesticks standing before the God of the earth." "10 And they

Who are the "Two Witnesses" of Rev. 11

> that dwell upon the earth shall rejoice over them, and make merry, and shall send gifts one to another; because these two prophets tormented them that dwelt on the earth." Revelation 11:3, 4, 10.

1). *The "two prophets"* _____ In the above comparative verses, of Revelation 11:3, 4, and 10, the "two olive trees and the two candlesticks" of v.4 are personified to "two witnesses," in v.3, and the "two witnesses" of v.3 are personified to "two prophets" in v.10.

Likewise, in Christ's predictions (Matthew 16:28), Jesus states that there would be more than one of His apostles (prophets) that would remain alive, by the use of the word "some" ("some standing here"). And these apostles (prophets) would remain alive standing on earth before Christ, "till they see the Son of man coming in His kingdom." Matthew 16:28

———

"11 And he said unto me, Thou [you] must prophesy again before many peoples, and nations, and tongues, and kings." Revelation 10:11

"3 And I will give power unto my two witnesses, and they shall prophesy a thousand two hundred and threescore days [3.5 years], clothed in sackcloth." Revelation 11:3

2). *"Thou [you] must prophesy again"* _____ In Revelation chapter eleven and verse three above, the angel of the LORD of hosts says that the "two prophets" ("two witnesses") were to "prophesy" publicly for 3.5 years "clothed in sackcloth," just before they were "killed" (Revelation 11:7).

Likewise, the two prophets ("some") of Christ the LORD of hosts (Matthew 16:28; Revelation 10:11) were to

Who are the "Two Witnesses" of Rev. 11

prophesy again before many peoples, and nations, and tongues, and kings" (Revelation 10:11), just before they were killed ("taste of death"). "28 There be some standing here, which shall not taste of death, **till** they see the Son of man coming in His kingdom." Matthew 16:28

In addition, Revelation eleven and verse three gives us the duration the two prophets of the LORD of hosts are going to prophesy, which is 3.5 years; and also v.3 reveals to us that the two prophets of the LORD would be clothed in "sackcloth" signifying that they are in mourning.

———

"28 Verily I say unto you, There be some standing here, which shall not taste of death, till they see the Son of man coming in His kingdom." Matthew 16:28

"22 Jesus saith unto him, If I will that he [Apostle John] tarry till I come, what is that to thee [you]? follow thou [you] Me." John 21:22

"5 And if any man will hurt them, fire proceedeth out of their mouth, and devoureth their enemies: and if any man will hurt them, he must in this manner be killed. 6 These have power to shut heaven, that it rain not in the days of their prophecy: and have power over waters to turn them to blood, and to smite the earth with all plagues, as often as they will." Revelation 11:4, 5

3). *Cannot be killed by human hands* _____ As you have read in Revelation eleven and verses four and five, the "two prophets" of the LORD of hosts cannot be killed by human hands as hard as they may try; instead, those who attempt to kill them, they are killed in the same manner they were trying to kill the two prophets of the LORD of hosts.

And as you have read in Matthew 16:28 and John 21:22, the "two prophets" of the LORD of hosts, also cannot be killed up on "till they see the Son of man coming in His kingdom."

Who are the "Two Witnesses" of Rev. 11

———

"28 Verily I say unto you, There be some standing here, which shall not taste of death, till they see the Son of man coming in His kingdom." Matthew 16:28

"7 And when they shall have finished their testimony, the beast that ascendeth out of the bottomless pit shall make war against them, and shall overcome them, and kill them." Revelation 11:7

4). *The "beast" kills the "two prophets"* _____ The angel of Christ the LORD of hosts affirmed that the "two prophets" of the LORD would be killed by "the beast" from "the bottomless pit" (Revelation 11:7). And then, the angel of the LORD of hosts gives us some gruesome detailed information in regards to the deaths of the two prophets of the LORD of hosts, by saying,

> "8 And their dead bodies [the two prophets] shall lie in the street of the great city, which spiritually is called Sodom and Egypt, where also our LORD was crucified.

> "9 And they of the people and kindreds and tongues and nations shall see their dead bodies three days and an half, and shall not suffer their dead bodies to be put in graves.

> "10 And they that dwell upon the earth shall rejoice over them, and make merry, and shall send gifts one to another; because these two prophets tormented them that dwelt on the earth." Revelation 11:8-10

Likewise, the two prophets of Matthew 16:28), although

Who are the "Two Witnesses" of Rev. 11

Jesus states that His two prophets ("some") "shall not taste of death, till they see the Son of man coming in His kingdom," He does say that they will "taste of death" when they do see the "Son of man coming in His kingdom" (Matthew 16:28).

———

"28 Verily I say unto you, There be some standing here, which shall not taste of death, till they see the Son of man coming in His kingdom." Matthew 16:28

"11 And after three days and an half the Spirit of life from God entered into them, and they stood upon their feet; and great fear fell upon them which saw them." Revelation 11:11

5).   *The "two prophets" resurrected* _____ In order for the two prophets of the LORD of hosts to be able to see "the Son of man coming into His kingdom" (Matthew 16:28), the two prophets of the LORD had to be resurrected (Matthew. 16:28); and that belief is also stated by the angel of the LORD when he said, "the Spirit of life from God entered into them [the two dead prophets], and they stood upon their feet" (Revelation 11:11).

———

"28 Verily I say unto you, There be some standing here, which shall not taste of death, till they see the Son of man coming in His kingdom." Matthew 16:28

"12 And they heard a great voice from heaven saying unto them, Come up hither. And they ascended up to heaven in a cloud; and their enemies beheld them." Revelation 11:12

6).   *The "two prophets" taken to heaven* _____ And when the two prophets were resurrected, "fear fell upon them which saw them." The wicked thought it was payback time for killing the two prophets. But to their relief, "12 they heard a great voice from heaven saying unto them [the two prophets], Come up

Who are the "Two Witnesses" of Rev. 11

hither. And they ascended up to heaven in a cloud; and their enemies beheld them." Revelation 11:12

————

Comparatively the "two prophets" of the LORD "see the Son of man coming in His kingdom" (Matthew 16:28) not only because they see and understand the prophetic events before them, but at the same time they can see the preparation of "the Son of man coming in His kingdom." Matthew 16:28

Here are some of the references:

"14 The second woe is past; and, behold, the third woe cometh quickly.

"15 And the seventh angel sounded; and there were great voices in heaven, saying, The kingdoms of this world are become the kingdoms of our Lord, and of his Christ; and He shall reign for ever and ever.

"16 And the four and twenty elders, which sat before God on their seats, fell upon their faces, and worshipped God, 17 Saying, We give thee [You] thanks, O LORD God Almighty, which art, and wast, and art to come; because thou [You] hast taken to thee [You] thy [Your] great power, and hast reigned." Revelation 11:14-17

7).   *The "two prophets" see Christ "coming in His kingdom"*
————— It should be noted, Christ the LORD of hosts states that at least two of His apostles ("prophets") will see Christ "coming" in "His kingdom." He does not say that Christ has come in His kingdom or received His kingdom. Christ the LORD simply states that at least two of His prophets ("some")

will "see the Son of man coming in His kingdom."

————

> "13 And the same hour was there a great earthquake, and the tenth part of the city fell, and in the earthquake were slain of men seven thousand: and the remnant were affrighted, and gave glory to the God of heaven." Revelation 11:13

8).   *The great earthquake* _____ According to the above verse, although the wicked were relieved that nothing happened to them, when the two prophets were resurrected; to their unexpected surprise, there was a devastating earthquake, which took place within the hour, from the time the two prophets of the LORD of hosts were taken to heaven to the time the earthquake shook the city of Jerusalem.

————

> "14 The second woe is past; and, behold, the third woe cometh quickly." Revelation 11:14

9).   As you have read in the above verse (v.14), once all of the events are fulfilled from the time the "second woe" begins (Revelation 9:12 and ends with the start of the "third woe" (Revelation 11:14 the seventh angel will sound his trumpet (Revelation 11:15).

But, you should know that chapters ten and eleven (Rev. 9:21 to 11:1-14) of the book of Revelation are wedged in between the "second woe" and the "third woe." And, if we separate the "second woe" from chapters ten, eleven, and the "third woe," we will have the following:

> "12 One woe is past; and, behold, there come two woes

more hereafter.

"13 And the sixth angel sounded, and I heard a voice from the four horns of the golden altar which is before God, 14 Saying to the sixth angel which had the trumpet, Loose the four angels which are bound in the great river Euphrates. 15 And the four angels were loosed, which were prepared for an hour, and a day, and a month, and a year, for to slay the third part of men.

"16 And the number of the army of the horsemen were two hundred thousand thousand [200 million]: and I heard the number of them. 17 And thus I saw the horses in the vision, and them that sat on them, having breastplates of fire, and of jacinth, and brimstone: and the heads of the horses were as the heads of lions; and out of their mouths issued fire and smoke and brimstone. 18 By these three was the third part of men killed, by the fire, and by the smoke, and by the brimstone, which issued out of their mouths. 19 For their power is in their mouth, and in their tails: for their tails were like unto serpents, and had heads, and with them they do hurt.

"20 And the rest of the men which were not killed by these plagues yet repented not of the works of their hands, that they should not worship devils, and idols of gold, and silver, and brass, and stone, and of wood: which neither can see, nor hear, nor walk:

"21 Neither repented they of their murders, nor of their sorceries, nor of their fornication, nor of their thefts."
Revelation 9:12-21

Who are the "Two Witnesses" of Rev. 11

As you have read in the above verses, the "second woe" follows the "first woe," which involves a chemical war in the Middle East that will not kill its victims but let them be tormented and suffer for five months (Rev. 9:5, 6); they will seek death but they will not be able to find it. Clearly, the "second woe" begins with Revelation 9:12 and end with v.21.

And, noticeably, chapters ten and part of eleven (10; 11:1-14) of Revelation are wedged in between the "second woe" (Rev. 9:21), and the "third woe" (Rev. 11:14, 15), which ends with Revelation 16:21

Consequentially, the events of chapter ten and part of chapter eleven are placed at the end of the "second woe" and at the beginning of the "third woe," which dictates a very short time period for the events of Chapters ten and eleven to be fulfilled. And that time period, if we were to calculate it, it will give Apostle John and his associate ("two prophets") a very short but coordinated time frame to accomplish their three and a half years mission in the city of Jerusalem.

Since Apostle John and his associate will eventually come to Jerusalem wearing "sackcloth" clothing, testifying, prophesying before the world scene for three and a half years, be killed by the "beast" at the end of the three and a half years, be resurrected after three and a half days, and the earthquake in Jerusalem taking place after Apostle John's and his associate's ascension to heaven, we can conclude that the whole time fame, before the "third woe" begins, is in the neighborhood of slightly over three and a half years.

The other point that should be remembered is the fact, although Apostle John and his associate will testify and prophesy before nations, kings, tongues, and kindred; their testimony and their messages and their counsel will be rejected by the wicked. We are told,

"20 And the rest of the men which were not killed by

Who are the "Two Witnesses" of Rev. 11

these plagues yet repented not of the works of their hands, that they should not worship devils, and idols of gold, and silver, and brass, and stone, and of wood: which neither can see, nor hear, nor walk: "21 Neither repented they of their murders, nor of their sorceries, nor of their fornication, nor of their thefts." Revelation 9:12-21

At this point, which is at the end of Apostle John's and his associate's "prophesying" and "testimony" and at the beginning of the "third woe," the seventh angel will sound.

By following the above sequential events of Revelation chapter eleven, we can see how the "two olive trees and the two candlesticks" are personified into human beings by saying they are going to "prophesy" for 3.5 years in Jerusalem, get killed, their dead bodies remain dead for 3.5 days, they are resurrected, and then, taken to heaven.

And, we can see the similarities in the events Apostle John and his associate are going to go through, and experience. After they reveal themselves to the world (Revelation 10:11), they are to "prophesy again" (besides his writings); they are going to personally "prophesy" at the end of the "second woe" before kindred, tongues, and nations. And they are going to "prophecy" at the end of the "2nd woe," before they are killed. And shortly after they are killed, they will remain dead for a while in order to "taste of death" (Matthew 16:28). After they "taste of death," Apostle John and his associate are going to be resurrected. And when the un-repentant wicked men and women see the two apostles resurrected, they watch in fear. And then, the two apostles are taken to heaven before the "third woe" begins to sound, in order to see Christ's coming "in His kingdom," fulfilling Christ's words when He said, "28 some standing here, which shall not taste of death, **till** they see the Son of man coming in His kingdom." Matthew 16:28

The Last Call to Repentance

Accordingly, the personified "two olive trees and the two candlesticks" of Revelation 11:3-12 coincide with Matthew 16:28; John 21:21, 22 and Rev. 10:11, matching the activities of Apostle John and his associate.

Therefore, as per the above presentation, we can conclude that the "two witnesses" (prophets of the LORD) of Revelation chapter eleven, Matthew 16:28; John 21:21, 22; Rev. 10:11) are referring to Apostle John and his associate. For that reason, henceforth I will address the "two witnesses," of Revelation chapter eleven, as Apostle John and his associate. (For more comparative info, see supplements.)

But, if you don't accept the fact that the "two olive trees and the two candlesticks" are personified, and represent Apostle John and his associate, then we can ask, what is the purpose of keeping Apostle John and his associate alive for all of these 2,000 years "till they see the Son of man coming in His kingdom"?

The Last Call to Repentance _____ The "two witnesses" (Apostle John and his associate) are given power to not only "prophesy" for 3.5 years in Jerusalem, but to also protect themselves, from those who desperately want to kill them, in order to stop them from proclaiming, to the wicked men, women, and children of age the last call to repentance.

Here is the reference:

> "3 And I will give power unto my two witnesses, and they shall prophesy a thousand two hundred and threescore days [3.5 years], clothed in sackcloth." Revelation 11:3

So! Why are the "two witnesses" (Apostle John and his associate) so un-destructively protected from the human hands of the wicked men and women?

The Last Call to Repentance

They are because Christ the LORD of hosts, in His mercy, wants Apostle John and his associate to testify for 3.5 years before kings, nations, tongues, and kindred, in order to give the entire human race the last call to repentance.

You see, in the sequence of the "prophecy" in the book of Revelation, after the "great tribulation" (Matthew 24:21; Revelation 13:11-18), in which we are living in, but more precisely, we are living in the second half of v.12, which reads,

> "12 And he [2nd beast; Britain & USA] exerciseth all the power of the first beast [Revelation 13:1-10 (pope)] before him, and causeth the earth and them which dwell therein to worship the first beast [pope], whose deadly wound was healed [Rev. 13:3]." Revelation 13:12

As you have read in the above verse, the second half of the verse says that the second beast (Britain and USA. v.11) is going to compel all of the people of planet earth to worship the 1st beast (the pope of Revelation 13:1-10, 18). And in the sequence of the "prophecy," "immediately" after the "great tribulation" is over, "the sign" of Christ's soon coming appears in heaven for all to see (Matthew 24:29, 30).

After "the sign" of Christ's second coming appears in heaven (Matt. 24:29, 30), and just before the plagues of Rev. 8 and 9 begin to fall, Christ's penitent people are sealed for eternal life (Revelation 7:1-4). And after Christ's penitent people are sealed, the seven plagues (Revelation 8 & 9) begin to fall upon the wicked and upon the ecosystem of the earth. (To view Revelation chapters 8 & 9, go to Supplements.)

But, when the "second woe" ends of Revelation chapter nine, Apostle John and his associate arrive in Jerusalem to testify, prophesy, and to give, for 3.5 years, to all of the people of the world, the last call to repentance.

The Last Call to Repentance

One of the reason why Jesus Christ the LORD of hosts wants Apostle John and his associate to give the last call to repentance is due to the fact that Jesus Christ in His mercy wants all of the repentant children who become of age, and know between right and wrong, to be saved. And of course, even adult stragglers who might have a change of heart.

These children are the ones who become aware of right and wrong after God's people were sealed (Rev. 7:1-4), and right up until the time Apostle John and his associate are killed by the beast from the bottomless pit (Revelation 11:7). These children are given the opportunity to repent, accept Jesus Christ as their LORD, God, and Savior, and be saved in His kingdom for eternity. Sending Apostle John and his associate to Jerusalem for 3.5 years is like giving the un-repentant sinners a second chance.

Jesus does not want to leave a single repentant sinner behind to perish. That is why the door of mercy will remain open right up until the last minute before probation closes, so that no one can say that they were not given ample time and the opportunity to be saved.

On the other hand, if the un-repented wicked men and women and children of age don't want to repent, Jesus Christ, in His mercy wants to reveal the extreme sinful evil the wicked are capable of becoming. And to prove to all of the created beings of the universe and outside of the universe, although man was created a little bit lower than the angels (Hebrews 2:7), Apostle John and his associate are still going to remain sinless, in an extreme wicked environment for 3.5 years, where sin is committed as far as the imagination of the wicked can take them.

Therefore, to those individuals who claim that man is incapable of keeping the 10 Commandments, as they are given in Exodus 20:2-17, is a complete lie.

In passing, let me remind you; the 10 Commandments

The Last Call to Repentance

(Exodus 20:2-17), as they were given to the children of Israel [Jacob], they were "to give unto us," the Gentiles (Acts 7:38).

Nonetheless, Apostle John and his associate remain sinless in an unholy environment, just as Enoch, Moses, Elijah, King David, Apostle Peter, etc., etc., and that means you can also remain sinless before Christ our Creator, if you truly want to? All you have to do is to accept Jesus Christ as your LORD, God, and Savior, confess your sins to Him, ask Him to forgive all of your sins, and you will be holy before Christ the LORD of hosts.

It does not matter how gruesome, horrid, perverted evil acts you have committed, Jesus Christ the LORD is always ready to forgive a penitent sinner's sins.

Therefore, since Apostle John and his associate will overcome sin during the 3.5 years of "testimony" in Jerusalem, you and I can overcome sin and be victorious over sin and sinful habits, which fester in our lives by which we are tempted by satanic agencies.

Just remember, we are not going to be tempted by satanic agencies more than we are able to bear. They are not allowed to tempt a penitent sinner more that he or she is able to bear.

The fact that Apostle John and his associate are taken to heaven after their 3.5 years of "testimony" is proof enough that they overcame sin and remain sinless before Christ the LORD of hosts. And since they are able to overcome sin and sinful temptations, you and I can do the same with the help of Jesus Christ our LORD.

Apostle Paul encourages;

"13 There hath no temptation taken you but such as is common to man: but God is faithful, who will not suffer you to be tempted above that ye [all of you] are able; but will with the

The Last Call to Repentance

temptation also make a way to escape, that ye
may be able to bear it." 1 Corinthians 10:13

According to the above verse, Satan and his satanic
agencies cannot tempt a human being more than he or she is
able to bear. And, there is a promise that every sinner on planet
earth will be able to overcome sinful habits and temptations; we
are told because Jesus Christ has overcome all manner of
temptations that befall human beings, we too can be victorious
over sinful temptations.

The apostle writes:

"18 For in that He [Jesus Christ the LORD of
hosts] Himself hath suffered being tempted, He
is able to succour them that are tempted."
Hebrews 2:18

The above statement by the apostle is very encouraging;
he says, Christ "is able to succour them that are tempted."

Did you hear that?

Jesus Christ can deliver the penitent sinner from
temptation. Therefore it does not matter to what degree the
temptation is volleyed upon sinners, they will be able to
overcome because Jesus Christ will be there to help the sinners
to overcome.

But, if sinners do not want to repent and choose to live
in sin, it does not matter what Jesus Christ says or what Apostle
John and his associate say to them, they will reject the Gospel
doctrine and pursue the lust of their sinful hearts and therefore
reject Apostle John's and his associate's testimony.

The prophet of the LORD of hosts writes:

"3 For the time will come when they will not
endure sound doctrine; but after their own lusts

The Last Call to Repentance

> shall they heap to themselves teachers, having
> itching ears; 4 And they shall turn away their
> ears from the truth, and shall be turned unto
> fables." 2 Timothy 4:3, 4

> "12 That they all might be damned who believed
> not the truth, but had pleasure in
> unrighteousness." 2 Thessalonians 2:12

After Apostle John and his associate finish their 3.5
years of testimony and prophesy in Jerusalem, just before the
"third woe" sounds, wicked men and women reject Apostle
John's and his associate's testimony; they choose to believe
"fables," and reject Jesus Christ as their LORD, God, and
Savior. And when they do, Satan (the Devil) takes over, and
starts a war with Apostle John and his associate. And when he
does, the people of Jerusalem will fervently get involved in
monitoring the fight; and at the same time, they will record the
blow by blow events with their cell-phones, video cameras,
radio stations, newspapers, computers, tablets, internet, and so
on will the molecular electronic terra-bites of information be
spread in the world arena that is going to be watching intently
of the outcome of the war.

And when Satan (the beast from the bottomless pit)
kills Apostle John and his associate, in their un-repented
mindset, the wicked men and women are relieved that finally
Apostle John's and his associate's demise had taken place. They
give Satan a hero's welcome and spread the news throughout
the world of the outcome of the war. And in their joyous hype,
they begin to celebrate the kill by giving each other gifts. The
prophet of the LORD writes; "10 And they that dwell upon the
earth shall rejoice over them, and make merry, and shall send
gifts one to another; because these two prophets tormented
them that dwelt on the earth." Revelation 11:10

The Last Call to Repentance

For three and a half days the wicked cajole each other with hyped malice towards the two prophets of the LORD and make fun of their dead bodies while they lay on the street to rot where they were killed in Jerusalem.

In their hyped frenzy of joy and happiness, they watch the dead bodies of the two prophets of the LORD decomposing, and each day for three and a half days, they ridiculed and make fun of the apostle's testimony and their prophecy and of their useless powers.

But, at the end of the three and a half days, Apostle John and his associate are resurrected by Jesus Christ the LORD of hosts. And, as they stretch their bodies and start walking, fear spreads upon those who are watching Apostle John and his associate walking about in the streets of Jerusalem. And as the news begins to spread, fear spreads also. The unrepentant inhabitants of Jerusalem and abroad think that retribution time has come upon them; but, to their surprise, they hear a voice from heaven saying to Apostle John and to his associate,

> "12 Come up hither. And they ascended up to heaven in a cloud; and their enemies beheld them." Revelation 11:12

Although the wicked were relieved that no retribution befall upon them, but, within the hour, after Apostle John and his associate were taken to heaven, an earthquake shatters one tenth of the city of Jerusalem and kills 7,000 people.

The prophet of the LORD of hosts writes:

> "13 And the same hour was there a great earthquake, and the tenth part of the city fell, and in the earthquake were slain of men seven thousand: and the remnant were affrighted, and

The Last Call to Repentance

gave   glory   to   the   God   of   heaven."
Revelation 11:13

Although the un-repentant wicked men and women give glory to God after the earthquake, unfortunately, it will not be because they love Christ the LORD of hosts; they will do it out of fear.

After the earthquake, Apostle John tells us that men and women will still remain proud, arrogant, worship devils, and defiantly wicked towards Christ the LORD of hosts,

Apostle John writes:

"20 And the rest of the men which were not killed by these plagues yet repented not of the works of their hands, that they should not worship devils, and idols of gold, and silver, and brass, and stone, and of wood: which neither can see, nor hear, nor walk:

"21 Neither repented they of their murders, nor of their sorceries, nor of their fornication, nor of their thefts." Revelation 9:20, 21

The status of evil men and women remain the same. They do not repent. They choose to serve Satan and his satanic agencies. They "21 Neither repented they of their murders, nor of their sorceries, nor of their fornication, nor of their thefts." Revelation 9:21

At that point in time, the "2nd woe" will pass, the 3.5 years of testimony and prophesying will be over, and after the earthquake takes place in Jerusalem, the "3rd woe" is come.

Here is the reference:

"14 The second woe is past; and, behold, the

The Last Call to Repentance

third woe cometh quickly." Revelation 11:14

And, as it was stated above, after the earthquake in the city of Jerusalem is over, the seventh angel will sound and the "third woe" will begin to be implemented.

Apostle John writes:

> "15 And the seventh angel sounded; and there were great voices in heaven, saying, The kingdoms of this world are become the kingdoms of our Lord, and of his Christ; and He shall reign for ever and ever." Revelation 11:15

Once the seventh angel sounds, and the "third woe" begins, the angels in heaven acknowledge that "the mystery of God should be finished" (Revelation 10:7), and utter the words that the kingdoms of planet earth have become "the kingdoms of our Lord, and of his Christ"; and when that is acknowledged by the hosts of heaven,

> "16 the four and twenty [24] elders, which sat before God on their seats, fell upon their faces, and worshipped God, "17 Saying, We give thee [You} thanks, O LORD God Almighty, which art, and wast, and art to come; because thou [You] hast taken to thee [You] thy [Your] great power, and hast reigned." Revelation 11:16, 17

Seeing that the wicked men and women realize that the two men of God the Christ have been taken to heaven and of the prophetic deadly coming events, many men and women begin to seek the word of God; but the word of God cannot be found. Neither are they able to hear "the word of the LORD."

The Last Call to Repentance

The prophet of the LORD of hosts writes:

"11 Behold, the days come, saith the LORD GOD, that I will send a famine in the land, not a famine of bread, nor a thirst for water, but of hearing the words of the LORD:

"12 And they shall wander from sea to sea, and from the north even to the east, they shall run to and fro to seek the word of the LORD, and shall not find it." Amos 8:11, 12

Many of the wicked men and women become conscious of the seriousness of the predicament they put themselves in; therefore they begin to wander in vain from place to place seeking the word of the LORD. Eventually, reality sits in, and then, anxiety follows with a grim panicky ordeal that there is no escape from the coming doom. Therefore the wicked blame God the Christ for their predicament; and in their hate towards Jesus Christ the LORD, they blaspheme His holy name with vengeance. And at that point in time, if Jesus Christ the LORD was down here on earth, they would take Him and re-crucify Him.

Therefore the wicked men and women throughout the world interact with each other and continue to blame Christ the LORD for not giving them another chance to repent. But, even if another chance were to be given to the un-repented evil hearts of men and women, they would do the same things all over again.

Would another three and a half years of testimony and counsel to the wicked men and women make a difference?

I doubt it?

And so does the prophet of Christ the LORD of hosts who wrote,

The Last Call to Repentance

"18 And the nations were angry, and thy [Your] wrath is come, and the time of the dead, that they should be judged, and that thou [You] shouldest give reward unto thy [Your] servants the prophets, and to the saints, and them that fear thy name, small and great; and shouldest destroy them which destroy the earth." Revelation 11:18

Although the nations are angry and hate Jesus Christ the LORD of hosts because He will not let them, Satan, or his evil angels continue to live on planet earth, in their sin filled environment; in the interim, Jesus Christ is getting ready to come to planet earth with His saints (angels), and to give the rewards to His dead and living saints (men, women, and children). But first, the "third woe" must take its course. Therefore, I will move forward, near the end of chapter fifteen; and in Revelation chapter fifteen, we have the following events documented.

Apostle John writes:

"5 And after that I looked, and, behold, the temple of the tabernacle of the testimony in heaven was opened:

"6 And the seven angels came out of the temple, having the seven plagues, clothed in pure and white linen, and having their breasts girded with golden girdles.

"7 And one of the four beasts gave unto the seven angels seven golden vials full of the wrath of God, who liveth for ever and ever.

"8 And the temple was filled with smoke from the glory of God, and from his power; and no man was able to

The Last Call to Repentance

enter into the temple, till the seven plagues of the seven angels were fulfilled." Revelation 15:5-8

As you have read in the above verses, the seven angels who came out of the heavenly Temple each received a vial that is filled with the wrath of God. And these seven angels are told to go on their way to planet earth and each angel is to pour the vials in succession upon the earth.

Apostle John says,

"1 And I heard a great voice out of the temple saying to the seven angels, Go your ways, and pour out the vials of the wrath of God upon the earth.

"2 And the first went, and poured out his vial upon the earth; and there fell a noisome and grievous sore upon the men which had the mark of the beast [pope], and upon them which worshipped his image [pope's political and pagan religious doctrine].

"3 And the second angel poured out his vial upon the sea; and it became as the blood of a dead man: and every living soul died in the sea.

"4 And the third angel poured out his vial upon the rivers and fountains of waters; and they became blood.

"5 And I heard the angel of the waters say, Thou [You] art righteous, O LORD, which art, and wast, and shalt be, because thou [You] hast judged thus.

"6 For they have shed the blood of saints and prophets, and thou [You] hast given them blood to drink; for they are worthy.

The Last Call to Repentance

The Last Call to Repentance

"7 And I heard another out of the altar say, Even so, LORD God Almighty, true and righteous are thy [Your] judgments.

"8 And the fourth angel poured out his vial upon the sun; and power was given unto him to scorch men with fire.

"9 And men were scorched with great heat, and blasphemed the name of God, which hath power over these plagues: and they repented not to give Him glory.

"10 And the fifth angel poured out his vial upon the seat of the beast [Vatican: Rev. 13:1, 2); and his kingdom was full of darkness; and they gnawed their tongues for pain,

"11 And blasphemed the God of heaven because of their pains and their sores, and repented not of their deeds.

"12 And the sixth angel poured out his vial upon the great river Euphrates; and the water thereof was dried up, that the way of the kings of the east might be prepared.

"13 And I saw three unclean spirits like frogs come out of the mouth of the dragon [Satan], and out of the mouth of the beast [pope], and out of the mouth of the false prophet [Muhammad].

"14 For they are the spirits of devils, working miracles, which go forth unto the kings of the earth and of the

The Last Call to Repentance

whole world, to gather them to the battle of that great day of God Almighty.

"15 Behold, I come as a thief. Blessed is he that watcheth, and keepeth his garments, lest he walk naked, and they see his shame.

"16 And he gathered them together into a place called in the Hebrew tongue Armageddon.

"17 And the seventh angel poured out his vial into the air; and there came a great voice out of the temple of heaven, from the throne, saying, **It is done**." Revelation 16:1-17

"11 He that is unjust, let him be unjust still: and he which is filthy, let him be filthy still: and he that is righteous, let him be righteous still: and he that is holy, let him be holy still." Revelation 22:11

"12 And, behold, I [Christ] come quickly; and My reward is with Me, to give every man according as his work shall be.

"13 I [Christ] am Alpha and Omega, the beginning and the end, the first and the last [Rev. 1:17, 18; Isaiah 44:6]." Revelation 22:12, 13

By Christ the LORD of hosts pronouncing the above decree (Revelation 22:11), the destiny of the human race will be sealed. The dead and the living will fall into two categories, holy and unholy, saved and unsaved. There is no turning back. The final plea to repentance was given for 3.5 years by Apostle Joan

The Last Call to Repentance

and his associate to the citizens of the world, and the un-repentant proud hearts of the wicked chose to remain unholy.

Apostle John writes,

> "20 yet repented not of the works of their hands, that they should not worship devils, and idols of gold, and silver, and brass, and stone, and of wood: which neither can see, nor hear, nor walk: 21 Neither repented they of their murders, nor of their sorceries, nor of their fornication, nor of their thefts" (Revelation 9:20, 21). (See also Revelation 16:9, 11, 21.)

As per the above verses, the wicked prefer to live in sin and continue to worship devils and not repent. Instead, they choose to curse Christ the God of Abraham, and repent not "of their murders, nor of their sorceries, nor of their fornication, nor of their thefts."

Therefore they find themselves under the un-protected hand of Jesus Christ the LORD, while the seven last deadly plagues fall upon the wicked and upon the ecosystem of the earth.

These seven last plagues, as you have read, are not partial, like the ones in chapters 8 & 9; they bring complete destruction upon the earth, upon human beings, and upon all life forms of the ecosystem. The dead bodies will be like dung left on the spot where they died because there will be no human being left alive to bury them; — can you imagine the chaos that will precede the dead?

Nonetheless, the prophet of the LORD writes,

> "18 And there were voices, and thunders, and lightnings; and there was a great earthquake, such as was not since men were upon the earth, so mighty an earthquake, and so great.

The Last Call to Repentance

"19 And the great city [Vatican] was divided into three parts, and the cities of the nations fell: and great Babylon [Vatican and her harlots. Revelation 17:5, 6] came in remembrance before God, to give unto her the cup of the wine of the fierceness of His wrath.

"20 And every island fled away, and the mountains were not found.

"21 And there fell upon men a great hail out of heaven, every stone about the weight of a talent [64 lbs]: and men blasphemed God because of the plague of the hail; for the plague thereof was exceeding great." Revelation 16:18-21

Meanwhile, as soon as the seventh angel pours upon the earth his vial that is full of the seventh plague, Jesus Christ the LORD God of Abraham, comes with all of His holy saints (angels) to planet earth, envelops the earth, parks way above the earth's atmosphere, and illuminates the earth from one end to the other end with greater brilliance than the sun. And when the people of planet earth see Jesus Christ, immediately there will be joy in the hearts of His repentant people. And immediately creating fear, anxiety, and agony for the wicked men and women causing them to flee and hide from the presence of Jesus Christ the LORD of hosts because the wicked know, if they look upon Christ's brilliance they will be destroyed (2 Thessalonians 2:8).

The prophet of the LORD writes:

"15 And the kings of the earth, and the great men, and the rich men, and the chief captains, and the mighty men, and every bondman, and every free man, hid themselves in the dens and

The Last Call to Repentance

in the rocks of the mountains;

"16 And said to the mountains and rocks, Fall on us, and hide us from the face of him that sitteth on the throne, and from the wrath of the Lamb:

"17 For the great day of His wrath is come; and who shall be able to stand?" Revelation 6:15-17

Although the wicked men and women scurry to go and hide from the presence of Christ the LORD God of His universe, Jesus Christ calls the sleeping (dead) saints (men and women and children) from their dusty and watery graves to awake and come forth (1 Corinthians 15:51-55). And at the same time, Christ the LORD of hosts resurrects a handful of wicked people who were involved during His crucifixion. (If you want more detailed information on the state of the dead read my book *"Ghosts Demons UFO'S and Dead Men"* By: Philip Mitanidis.)

Moreover, we are told,

"7 Behold, He [Christ] cometh with clouds; and every eye shall see Him, and they also which pierced Him: and all kindreds of the earth shall wail because of him. Even so, Amen." Revelation 1:7

As you have read in the above verse, the wicked who were involved in orchestrating Christ's death on Calvary's cross, and those individuals who took part in His crucifixion, they are going to be resurrected at Christ's 2nd coming, and remain alive (Revelation 1:7) to suffer the deadly seventh plague. After they receive the seventh plague, they are going to die for the second time; and then, wait to receive their final

The Last Call to Repentance

reward during their second resurrection, which it will be the first resurrection for the rest of the wicked dead. And during that resurrection, they are all going to receive their reward, which will be their eternal demise (Malachi 4:1-3).

And, if I may add; although all of those individuals who plotted Christ's crucifixion are going to be resurrected and receive the seventh deadly plague, there will be others who are not readily talked about in the Christian circles, which will also be resurrected during the time of the seven last plagues, and will receive the seven deadly plagues for adding, deleting, and misrepresenting the book of Revelation.

We are told:

> "18 For I testify unto every man that heareth the words of the prophecy of this book [book of Revelation], If any man shall add unto these things, God shall add unto him the plagues that are written in this book:"

And, in addition to the above warning, we are told,

> "19 And if any man shall take away from the words of the book of this prophecy, God shall take away his part out of the book of life, and out of the holy city, and from the things which are written in this book." Revelation 18, 19

So! If a man or a woman adds unto the words of the book of Revelation, "God shall add unto him the plagues that are written in this book." And, if any man or woman deletes any portion of the words of the prophecy, which is in the book of Revelation, we are told, "19 God shall take away his part out of the book of life, and out of the holy city, and from the things which are written in this book."

The Last Call to Repentance

Therefore, in order for a person to receive the last plagues for adding words to the book of Revelation or deleting words from the book of Revelation, Christ is going to resurrect these individuals, just like the individuals who crucified Jesus Chris the LORD. Consequently, be careful what you do with the words of the book of Revelation and with Jesus Christ the LORD of hosts.

Nonetheless, after the wicked who had part in Christ's crucifixion receive their reward, and those who add and delete words from the book of Revelation, Christ sends His holy angels who are hovering above the earth to gather all of His penitent people and bring them up out of the earth (Matthew 13:38-43; 25:41), and get ready to go to the third heaven, which is outside of Christ's universe.

And, as soon all of the dead saints and the living saints are redeemed from planet earth and secured with Christ's holy angels, the seventh deadly plague will continue to hammer the earth with about 64 lbs. of hail. Meanwhile, Christ, the redeemed, and His holy angels will begin their journey to their heavenly home. And when they do, their movement erupts the stable gravitational pull of the earth, in relationship to the sun and to the other planets. The young sun stops shining, and the earth goes into destructive convulsion in the dark cold space it occupies.

The prophet of the LORD of hosts writes:

"18 And it shall come to pass, that he who fleeth from the noise of the fear shall fall into the pit; and he that cometh up out of the midst of the pit shall be taken in the snare: for the windows from on high are open, and the foundations of the earth do shake.

"19 The earth is utterly broken down, the earth is clean dissolved, the earth is moved exceedingly.

The Last Call to Repentance

"20 The earth shall reel to and fro like a drunkard, and shall be removed like a cottage; and the transgression thereof shall be heavy upon it; and it shall fall, and not rise again." Isaiah 24:18-20

Although the earth suffers because of sin, as the above verses indicate; it will not remain uninhabitable for long, and a casualty because man chose to be a reckless steward.

Nonetheless, as a result of the above report, the mission of Apostle John and his associate is going to be accomplished. Apostle John will "prophesy again." The last call to repentance will be given for 3.5 years. It will be heralded from Jerusalem throughout the world; and decisions will be made by men and women for eternal life or for eternal death; and when the final decision is made, probation closes. The human race will seal its destiny before the seven last plagues (Rev. 16) begin to fall upon the wicked and upon the ecosystem of the earth.

But, before the seven last plagues begin to fall upon the earth, upon the wicked men, women, Satan, and his evil angels, and just before the lights go out (sun stops shining), can you imagine the possibilities of the various scenarios that can take place from the verses of Revelation chapter eleven?

A possible scenario.

Imagine the "two prophets" of the LORD of hosts (Apostle John and his associate), in the near coming closing events of the earth's history, arriving at a checkpoint in one of the borders of Israel dressed in sackcloth clothing for the sole purpose to "prophesy" in Jerusalem for 3.5 years.

What would the authorities think when they first lay their eyes upon them? I am sure besides analyzing them and their clothes, their brains would probably work, faster than 186,000 miles per second, filled with all sort of questions before they even begin to check their papers or their passports. And more than likely the border guards would keep an eye upon them, and look at them suspiciously, and wonder if they were carrying weapons underneath their sackcloth loosely fit garments? But they do not have to wonder very long because they already have focused their electronic scanning devices upon them to see if there is anything strapped upon their bodies that would be a detriment to the officers, and to those standing in the area. Since the scanners do not reveal anything that looks like a bomb or a weapon, Apostle John and his associate are cautiously motioned by the border guards to approach them. And when they do, the border guards take them aside and begin to physically search them, and question them, while the other border guards wait for answers from the local and the world database to confirm their identity?

The scenario could go a number of ways while the authorities hold Apostle John and his associate in custody. The paperwork and the passports could reveal that they are from another country, and make the authorities wonder how these two men were able to come this far through the borders of the other countries without being detained in those other countries because their paperwork is not up to date.

In another scenario, it could very well be that the

A Possible Scenario

paperwork would reveal that they are citizens of Jerusalem.

And that would also spark a number of serious questions. How were Apostle John and his associate able to leave Israel and travel to other countries and be able to come back with these old papers and passports?

In either case, Apostle John and his associate would run into un-welcomed relentless problems with the border guards because their papers and their passports are not acceptable and therefore they would not be allowed entry into the country. And even more bewildering and curious, how were these two men able to travel together without the "mark of the beast" (pope), in their right hands, without a tracking device (IC) in their right hands, or without the name of the beast whose number (666) in their right hands? Therefore, the authorities automatically detain them for further questioning.

And in regards to the "mark of the beast," if you are not familiar with the verses of "the mark of the beast," here are some of the references:

> "16 And he causeth all, both small and great, rich and poor, free and bond, to receive a mark in their right hand, or in their foreheads:

> "17 And that no man might buy or sell, save he that had the mark, or the name of the beast, or the number of his name.

> "18 Here is wisdom. Let him that hath understanding count the number of the beast: for it is the number of a man [pope]; and his number is Six hundred threescore and six [666]." Revelation 13:16-17

In view of the fact that Apostle John and his associate

A Possible Scenario

look like they were dressed in such weird attire, and look like they came out from a page somewhere in antiquity, and they have not received "the mark of the beast [pope]," or the tracking device (IC) in their right hands, the authorities keep them in custody till further notice from their superiors. (If you need more information on the "mark of the beast," read my book called *The Sign in Matthew 24* By: Philip Mitanidis.)

In the interim, the border guards receive a phone call from their superiors telling them that they were to take two officers, bind the two men with the weird clothing, and transport them to the processing facilities in Jerusalem.

Defensibly and cautiously the border guards secure Apostle John and his associate and vigilantly escort them to a guarded vehicle and put them in it. Then the two officers go into the vehicle, and drive away carefully, watching for the unexpected attack that might come upon them, and perhaps manage to free the two prisoners. And when they eventually reach the processing facilities in Jerusalem; the two officers hand over the two handcuffed men to the authorities.

The authorities take the men into the interrogation room and start to ask them questions; who are you? Why are you dressed like that? Why have you come to Israel? Why have you not received the "mark of the beast"? How were you able to travel into different countries without the "mark of the beast," and without the implant of the chip (IC) in their right hands, and, if they worshipped "the beast," why not, if they are Christians, are there others like them hiding and living in Israel, and so on the questions would continue to be asked.

Not having "the mark of the beast" or the implant of a tracking device in their right hands made the authorities wonder how Apostle John and his associate were able to hide from the international authorities for such a long time? But, more importantly, how were they able to sustain themselves since they, by law, were not able to buy food, water, shelter,

A Possible Scenario

and other commodities to sustain themselves without "the mark of the beast"?

When asked, if they would receive the mark of the beast and a tracking device, they refuse to receive the mark, or the number of the beast's name (666), or a chip in their right hands, they refuse! And that refusal made Apostle John and his associate enemies of the state. And under the civil religious and political laws of the land, Apostle John and his associate had to receive the mark or the implant of the tracking device in their right hands or face the death penalty.

Here is the reference:

> "15 And he [the 2nd best: Britain & USA] had power to give life unto the image [the pope's pagan religious & political doctrine] of the beast [pope], that the image of the beast should both speak, and cause that as many as would not worship the image of the beast [pope] should be killed." Revelation 13:15

The death penalty, as you have read in the above verse would be implemented during "the great tribulation" and enforced by the pope, Britain, and USA (Revelation 13:11-18), throughout the world by civil law; and if any man, woman, or child refused to worship the pope (of Revelation 13:1-10, 15, 18), and his political and pagan religious doctrine, which is masked under the name of Christianity that nonconformist would be killed by law.

What happened to the British Charter of rights, which gave us freedom to worship, human rights, freedom of speech, and to the American Constitution that was oh so meticulously written for the human race, and reverently celebrated, and held to be precious by our forefathers?

How did the mentors, who are behind the religious leaders, and political leaders, of England and USA, able to

A Possible Scenario

influence the leaders of the world to agree and pass the death penalty, in a so-called democratic system, upon the nonconformist is going to be a wake up call for the whole world? And, how democratic leaders of the entire world allow, by law, to implement "the mark of the beast" or an implant in "the right hand" upon all people of the world, with the exception of the nonconformists who are going to be identified as the enemies of state, is also going to be a wake up call for many people of the world, and a subject of discussion. They are going to wonder how did they allow the mentors, who are the instigators behind the politicians and behind the religious leaders, to pull wool over their eyes so deceitfully?

And given that the arrival of Apostle John and his associate are going to remain in Jerusalem for three and a half years in between the "second woe" and the "third woe," during the fulfillment of "the prophecy" of the book of Revelation, the authorities would be thinking, Apostle John and his associate should have received "the mark of the beast" in their right hands long, long time ago. But in view of the fact that they did not have a tracking device in their right hands, the authorities of Israel get suspicious of Apostle John and his associate, and keep them under close scrutiny. Since both men do not have tracking devices implanted in their right hands, the authorities would also be thinking that Apostle John and his associate might want to come out of hiding, give their allegiance to the pope, and receive the tracking devices in order to be able to get jobs, buy food, and get accommodations (Rev. 13:16-18). And perhaps reveal how they were able to survive for such a long time and avoid to be captured by the authorities.

But, when Apostle John and his associate are called to be processed with the "mark of the beast," they refuse the implants of the tracking devices in their right hands and they also refuse to impart any information in regards to Christ's

A Possible Scenario

penitent people. In doing so, the authorities immediately go on the defensive mode and think of the worst scenario possible that the two men are capable of doing covertly. But, since the two prophets of Christ the LORD of hosts (Apostle John and his associate) do not have any weapons, the authorities seize the moment and restrain them and lock them up and make ready for their public execution before the citizens of Jerusalem.

Once the authorities in Jerusalem, agree on the type of execution; they get busy immediately with their staff to contact the radio stations, the TV station, the newspapers, and all manner of advertising companies to advertise the date and time when the two men are going to be executed under the law. And when Apostle John and his associate are brought forward to be executed, they see a bloodthirsty humongous crowd waiting for them, and the news media focusing upon their every move. And when the crowd sees them, they delight in anticipation to see their deaths taking place.

This evil scene brought memories to Apostle John and his associate of Jesus Christ their LORD, God, and Savior when 2,000 years ago, after 3.5 years of ministry to the House of Judah (Jews), Jesus was brought before Pilate to be judged. The crowd, hyped by the priests and scribe and elders of the people, were screaming into the ears of Pilate, "crucify Him," "crucify Him," "crucify Him."

> "11 He [Christ] came unto His own, and His own [the House of Judah] received Him not." John 1:11

Instead, they killed Him!

Apostle John writes: "11 He came unto His own, and His own received Him not." John 1:11

Can you imagine killing the Creator of the universe?

A Possible Scenario

Similarly now, the crowd sees Apostle John and his associate as criminals because they would not conform to the dictates of "the beast." Therefore they are viewed as their enemies and worthy of death. Hence, they rejoice in the execution of the two prophets of Christ the LORD. But, when the authorities and the executioners try to make Apostle John and his associate an example to the onlookers and try to kill them, the executioners die the death they were implementing upon Apostle John and his associate. And when the jeering crowed in Jerusalem and throughout the world saw what happened to the executioners, they all gasped in awe and went into fearful silence.

Fear spread throughout Jerusalem upon the crowd and upon those who were watching through their electronic gadgetry; and wondered what kind of power these two men have to cause such an execution upon their executioners without lifting their hands upon them?

But, when some of the authorities saw what happened to the executioners, in their confusion, they quickly commanded the officers to grab the two prophets of the LORD, and contain them. But because the officers saw their colleagues die in front of their eyes, they blamed Apostle John and his associate for their deaths; and therefore, they brutally restrained them by hitting them with their clubs, punches, kicks, and so on. And as the punches, kicks, and clubs struck their victims, those who were delivering the blows to the two prophets of the LORD, progressively realized that the blows upon the two prophets of the LORD were delivered upon themselves. Realizing that their acts of brutality upon the LORD'S prophets were transferred upon themselves, the authorities thought that the two prophets of the LORD beat them up. And in order to prevent their escape, the authorities ordered that the two men be shot quickly right there on the spot. Although some were hesitant to shoot, but those that did,

A Possible Scenario

died by the bullets they fired upon Apostle John and his associate.

At this point, the recipients of the news, and the onlookers were shocked to see the events unfolding before their eyes; and wondered, how are these two men, from antiquity, able to protect themselves from bullets, beatings, and death?

And as the people that surrounded them, fearfully contemplated on the events before them, Apostle John and his associate reveal themselves to the masses; and then, they commence to witness for Christ the LORD of hosts. In doing so, the people immediately begin to hate their message and them, and all the more looked for ways to kill them. And when the wicked try to hurt them, they would be hurt the same way the wicked intended to hurt Apostle John and his associate. And when the wicked refuse to give Apostle John and his associate water to drink, Apostle John and his associate make the water of the wicked undrinkable by turning it into blood. And when snipers try to kill them, the snipers died right on the spot with their own bullets. And when the wicked try to kill them by throwing grenades upon them, the throwers died by the same grenades they threw upon the prophets of the LORD. And when the wicked fire a hand held missile upon Apostle John and his associate, the missile throwers died from the explosion of the same missile they fired upon Apostle John and his associate. And to make the wicked stop firing upon Apostle John and his associate, Apostle John and his associate, from time to time would smite the wicked with plagues at will and as often as they will. And sometimes, when the wicked would not stop their vicious deadly attacks upon them, Apostle John and his associate would bring fire upon their enemies and devour them in front of the onlookers.

As you have read earlier in the above verses, the "two witnesses" (Apostle John and his associate) will be harassed,

A Possible Scenario

intimidated, provoked, hurt, hated, and probably even put a bounty upon them to capture them, get rid of them, and even kill them if they can.

So, why are the wicked so bent on killing them?

They are because they do not want Apostle John and his associate preaching in the name of Jesus Christ the LORD; and perhaps hearing what the "seven thunders" (Revelation 10:4) had said, or what message or messages the "little book" (Revelation 10:9) has for them. Or, the wicked do not want the two witnesses revealing their wicked evil acts!

But, more to the point, the wicked want to kill Apostle John and his associate because they hate them and they hate Jesus Christ and they hate the messages and their prophecy so badly that it "torments" the wicked to no end (Revelation 11:10). Therefore the wicked want Apostle John and his associate out of Jerusalem, to put a lid upon their "testimony," and upon their "prophecy."

And to make matters even worse, the un-Godly citizens of Jerusalem, possibly, those that were not aware of the fact that the "two witnesses" (Apostle John and his associate) were not only going to stay in Jerusalem, but at the same time, they were going to preach to the people for three and a half years. Unfortunately, those three and a half years would aggravate the wickedness of the depraved relentlessly. But because the wicked men and women will not be able to hurt or kill Apostle John and his associate ("two witnesses"), at the end of the 3.5 years, the "beast" from the bottomless pit takes the task upon himself to go and do battle with them. Eventually the beast from the bottomless pit overpowers Apostle John and his associate, and kills them.

Here is the reference:

"7 And when they shall have finished their testimony, [after 3.5 years] the beast that

A Possible Scenario

ascendeth out of the bottomless pit shall make
war against them, and shall overcome them, and
kill them." Revelation 11:7

Did you notice, for three and a half years the people in
Jerusalem were not able to get rid of, discourage, or kill Apostle
John and his associate. But because the people in Jerusalem
were not able to kill Apostle John and his associate, when
Apostle John and his associate "finished their testimony," at
the end of the three and a half years, then in his fury, the beast
(Satan or one of his minions) from the bottomless pit was
allowed to make war with the "two witnesses" (Apostle John
and his associate), overcome them, "and kills them."

And when Satan kills Apostle John and his associate, he
leaves their dead bodies right there on the spot where he killed
them, in one of the streets of Jerusalem, for every one to see
his twisted evil handy-work.

Here is the reference:

"8 And their dead bodies shall lie in the street of
the great city, which spiritually is called Sodom
and Egypt, where also our LORD [Jesus Christ]
was crucified." Revelation 11:8

Although the authorities and the residence of Jerusalem
and the vast numbers who came to Jerusalem to see the
exposed and uncovered dead bodies of Apostle John and his
associate, in the street, no one makes the effort to take their
dead bodies and bury them.

We are told:

"9 And they of the people and kindreds and
tongues and nations shall see their dead bodies
three days and an half, and shall not suffer their

A Possible Scenario

> dead bodies to be put in graves." Revelation
> 11:9

As you have read, the dead bodies of Apostle John and his associate are going to be left in one of the streets of Jerusalem for three and a half days. During that time their bodies would be full of maggots eating their flesh; and at the same time their bodies would also begin to stink severely. And yet, no one took the time to even cover their dead bodies to prevent the people from viewing their gruesome deaths.

When Satan kills Apostle John and his associate, the people from Jerusalem are going to turn the apostle's deaths into a festive exhibition. In fact, according to the prophecy, the people from Jerusalem are going to be very happy to see Apostle John and his associate defeated and killed. And when the people throughout the world find out that Satan killed Apostle John and his associate, they to rejoice and make merry.

Here is the reference:

> "10 And they that dwell upon the earth shall
> rejoice over them, and make merry, and shall
> send gifts one to another; because these two
> prophets tormented them that dwelt on the
> earth." Revelation 11:10

And "they that dwell upon the earth," Apostle John writes, "shall rejoice over them [Apostle John and his associate]."

It must have been de ja vous to Apostle John writing about his death and then, experiencing it?

Did you notice, the prophet of the LORD refers to the dwellers upon the earth as "they." They are the ones who will, at that time, rejoice over the apostle's deaths and make merry and send gifts to each other.

A Possible Scenario

Can you picture the joyous hype around the world over the deaths of Apostle John and his associate?

That is quite an overwhelming affect their dead bodies will have over the evil tormentors of the world.

The deaths of these two prophets will bring joy to the evil un-repented hearts of men and women who hate Christ's repentant people, His prophets, and Jesus Christ the LORD of hosts (Exodus 20:5).

But their rejoicing is short lived because after three days and a half, the spirit of life from God the Christ inters into their dead bodies and Apostle John and his associate stand up on their two feet. And when they do, fear plagues those individuals who saw them standing in the street.

Here is the reference:

> "11 And after three days and an half the Spirit of life from God entered into them, and they stood upon their feet; and great fear fell upon them which saw them." Revelation 11:11

Can you imagine the anxiety, fear, and the buzz that will overtake Jerusalem, even the world? Every radio station, every TV station, every news paper, every coffee shop, every restaurant, every web page, every cell phone and whatever other electronic gadget that would exist at that time period will most likely be full with speculation, fear, anxiety, etc., etc. because now that the two prophets (Apostle John and his associate) are alive, people would start to think that it is retribution time for killing them. Therefore they would be expecting a grater reprisal to come upon them because they think the two prophets of the LORD are prepared to do battle again with Satan and defeat him. And when they do, what is going to happen to them?

But, as the wicked men, women, evil angels, and Satan

A Possible Scenario

look intently upon Apostle John and his associate, they hear a voice from heaven "saying unto them, Come up hither. And they ascended up to heaven in a cloud."

And when the crowd saw Apostle John and his associate ascending out of sight into heaven, they were relieved.

Here is the reference:

"12 And they heard a great voice from heaven saying unto them, Come up hither. And they ascended up to heaven in a cloud; and their enemies beheld them." Revelation 11:12

And, as soon as Apostle John and his associate went out of sight, the news media and chat rooms began to post, throughout the world, the news of their departure. Although the wicked did not know what to make of their departure, at least they knew that the "two witnesses" (Apostle John and his associate) were gone to heaven, and hoping that they do not return again. This time around, the wicked did not send gifts to each other to celebrate the apostle's departure. Instead they were wondering what would happen next, if anything of the things Apostle John and his associate prophesied?

And, as the wicked went about their business, within the hour of Apostle John and his associate ascending to heaven, "a great earthquake" shook Jerusalem and "the tenth part of the city fell" into ruins and "seven thousand men" were slain. And upon the rest of the people in Jerusalem, fear fell upon them.

Here is the reference:

"13 And the same hour was there a great earthquake, and the tenth part of the city fell, and in the earthquake were slain of men seven thousand: and the remnant were affrighted, and

A Possible Scenario

gave glory to the God of heaven." Revelation 11:13

But, after giving glory and acknowledgement "to the God of heaven," how quickly, after the above catastrophe, the wicked men and women resorted to their evil perverted acts, saying to God,

> "14 Therefore they say unto God, Depart from us; for we desire not the knowledge of thy [your] ways." Job 21:14

> "11 And for this cause God shall send them strong delusion, that they should believe a lie: 12 That they all might be damned who believed not the truth, but had pleasure in unrighteousness." 2 Thessalonians 2:11, 12

And because the wicked of the world refuse to repent and be saved in Christ's Kingdom, and live in righteousness, when the seven plagues are unleashed by the angels and begin to fall upon the wicked men and women and upon the ecosystem of the world, the wicked reveal their true character by blaspheming God for their plight.

Here are few references:

> "9 And men were scorched with great heat, and blasphemed the name of God, which hath power over these plagues: and they repented not to give Him glory.

> "10 And the fifth angel poured out his vial upon the seat of the beast; and his kingdom was full of darkness; and they gnawed their tongues for

A Possible Scenario

pain,

"11 And blasphemed the God of heaven because of their pains and their sores, and repented not of their deeds.

"17 And the seventh angel poured out his vial into the air; and there came a great voice out of the temple of heaven, from the throne, saying, It is done.

"18 And there were voices, and thunders, and lightnings; and there was a great earthquake, such as was not since men were upon the earth, so mighty an earthquake, and so great.

"19 And the great city [Vatican] was divided into three parts, and the cities of the nations fell: and great Babylon [Vatican and her "harlots" – supporters. (See Rev. 17:5, 6.)] came in remembrance before God, to give unto her the cup of the wine of the fierceness of His wrath.

"20 And every island fled away, and the mountains were not found.

"21 And there fell upon men a great hail out of heaven, every stone about the weight of a talent [64 lbs.]: and men blasphemed God because of the plague of the hail; for the plague thereof was exceeding great." Revelation 16:9-11, 17-21

As you have read in the above verses, the wicked of planet earth do not have a change of heart. They continue to

A Possible Scenario

live in wickedness because they "delight in unrighteousness."

Therefore, they hate a holy God; and they do not want to live with Him in "righteousness."

But, at this point, let me clarify an important fact; as you recall, Apostle John and his associate will "prophesy" for 3.5 years, get killed, and taken to heaven. And when the seventh angels sounds his trumpet "the temple was filled with smoke from the glory of God [Christ], and from His power; and no man was able to enter into the temple" (Revelation 15:8), by prayer, or by any other means. In other words, probation is over, evil men and women of planet earth have made their choice. Therefore, God the Holy Spirit will not take or send any more prayers to the heavenly Temple for Jesus Christ the LORD to mediate for them because there are no more repentant sinners seeking forgiveness and eternal life. Therefore "no man was able to enter into the temple."

> "14 The second woe is past; and, behold, the third woe cometh quickly.

> "15 And the seventh angel sounded; and there were great voices in heaven, saying, The kingdoms of this world are become the kingdoms of our Lord, and of his Christ; and He shall reign for ever and ever." Revelation 11:14, 15

> "8 And the temple was filled with smoke from the glory of God [Christ], and from His power; and no man was able to enter into the temple, till the seven plagues of the seven angels were fulfilled." Revelation 15:8

Although probation closes for the human race, as it is

A Possible Scenario

stated in the above verse, "no man was able to enter into the temple" (v.8), the final cut off point does not take place until Revelation 16:17 when Jesus says, "it is done." And when Jesus says, "it is done," He utters the decree saying,

> "11 He that is unjust, let him be unjust still: and he which is filthy, let him be filthy still: and he that is righteous, let him be righteous still: and he that is holy, let him be holy still." Revelation 22:11

Christ in Revelation sixteen and verse seventeen says, "it is done." The last call to repentance is over. Men and women have made their choices, for eternal life or for eternal death.

Now it is time to resurrect the righteous penitent men, women, and children from their death beads. Christ comes with His saints (angels: 1 Thessalonians 3:13) to planet earth, resurrects His people, sends His angels (Matthew 16:27; 13:49, 50; 24:31) to gather His saints who were dead and also gathers His saints that are alive and takes them all to the third heaven.

Apostle Paul says,

> "15 For this we say unto you by the word of the LORD, that we which are alive and remain unto the coming of the LORD shall not prevent them which are asleep [dead].

> "16 For the LORD Himself shall descend from heaven with a shout, with the voice of the archangel, and with the trump of God: and the dead in Christ shall rise first:

> "17 Then we which are alive and remain shall be

A Possible Scenario

caught up together with them in the clouds, to meet the LORD in the air: and so shall we ever be with the LORD." 1 Thessalonians 4:15-17

And, as Christ, the holy angels, and the redeemed move away from planet earth, the sun stops shining, all life forms in their agony begin to parish. Planet earth goes into convulsion, and begins to swing to and fro like a drunkard in

the cold, cold dark space it occupies waiting for the next prophetic event to take place.

"19 The earth is utterly broken down, the earth is clean dissolved, the earth is moved exceedingly.

"20 The earth shall reel to and fro like a drunkard, and shall be removed like a cottage; and the transgression thereof shall be heavy upon it; and it shall fall, and not rise again." Isaiah 24:19, 20

A Possible Scenario

  Jesus Christ the LORD of hosts in His mercy and love for the human race does not want any person to perish. He proved that point on Calvary's cross. For that reason, Jesus Christ has sent Apostle John and his associate on a mission of mercy in which they are to land in Jerusalem, near the end of their mission, for 3.5 years, in order to give the last call for repentance to perishing men and women of planet earth; and help them to choose eternal life. But, at that time of 3.5 years of the last call to repentance, if men and women willfully refuse eternal life, what more could Christ do?

  "20 He which testifieth these things saith, Surely I come quickly. Amen. Even so, come, LORD Jesus.

"21 The grace of our LORD Jesus Christ be with you all. Amen." Revelation 22:20, 21

Revelation 11 (OKJV)

"1 And there was given me a reed like unto a rod: and the angel stood, saying, Rise, and measure the temple of God, and the altar, and them that worship therein.

2 But the court which is without the temple leave out, and measure it not; for it is given unto the Gentiles: and the holy city shall they tread under foot forty and two months.

3 And I will give power unto my two witnesses, and they shall prophesy a thousand two hundred and threescore days, clothed in sackcloth.

4 These are the two olive trees, and the two candlesticks standing before the God of the earth.

5 And if any man will hurt them, fire proceedeth out of their mouth, and devoureth their enemies: and if any man will hurt them, he must in this manner be killed.

6 These have power to shut heaven, that it rain not in the days of their prophecy: and have power over waters to turn them to blood, and to smite the earth with all plagues, as often as they will.

7 And when they shall have finished their testimony, the beast that ascendeth out of the bottomless pit shall make war against them, and shall overcome them, and kill them.

8 And their dead bodies shall lie in the street of the great city, which spiritually is called Sodom and Egypt, where also our Lord was crucified.

9 And they of the people and kindreds and tongues and nations shall see their dead bodies three days and an half, and shall not suffer their dead bodies to be put in graves.

10 And they that dwell upon the earth shall rejoice over them, and make merry, and shall send gifts one to another; because these two prophets tormented them that dwelt on the earth.

11 And after three days and an half the Spirit of life from God

Revelation 11 (OKJV)

entered into them, and they stood upon their feet; and great fear fell upon them which saw them.

12 And they heard a great voice from heaven saying unto them, Come up hither. And they ascended up to heaven in a cloud; and their enemies beheld them.

13 And the same hour was there a great earthquake, and the tenth part of the city fell, and in the earthquake were slain of men seven thousand: and the remnant were affrighted, and gave glory to the God of heaven.

14 The second woe is past; and, behold, the third woe cometh quickly.

15 And the seventh angel sounded; and there were great voices in heaven, saying, The kingdoms of this world are become [the kingdoms] of our Lord, and of his Christ; and he shall reign for ever and ever.

16 And the four and twenty elders, which sat before God on their seats, fell upon their faces, and worshipped God,

17 Saying, We give thee thanks, O Lord God Almighty, which art, and wast, and art to come; because thou hast taken to thee thy great power, and hast reigned.

18 And the nations were angry, and thy wrath is come, and the time of the dead, that they should be judged, and that thou shouldest give reward unto thy servants the prophets, and to the saints, and them that fear thy name, small and great; and shouldest destroy them which destroy the earth.

19 And the temple of God was opened in heaven, and there was seen in his temple the ark of his testament: and there were lightnings, and voices, and thunderings, and an earthquake, and great hail." Revelation 11:1-19

Is Apostle John Still Alive Today *By: Philip Mitanidis*..........194
Supplements

Supplements
Revelation Chapters 8 & 9 (OKJV)

Revelation 8

1 And when he had opened the seventh seal, there was silence in heaven about the space of half an hour.

2 And I saw the seven angels which stood before God; and to them were given seven trumpets.

3 And another angel came and stood at the altar, having a golden censer; and there was given unto him much incense, that he should offer it with the prayers of all saints upon the golden altar which was before the throne.

4 And the smoke of the incense, which came with the prayers of the saints, ascended up before God out of the angel's hand.

5 And the angel took the censer, and filled it with fire of the altar, and cast it into the earth: and there were voices, and thunderings, and lightnings, and an earthquake.

6 And the seven angels which had the seven trumpets prepared themselves to sound.

7 The first angel sounded, and there followed hail and fire mingled with blood, and they were cast upon the earth: and the third part of trees was burnt up, and all green grass was burnt up.

8 And the second angel sounded, and as it were a great mountain burning with fire was cast into the sea: and the third part of the sea became blood;

9 And the third part of the creatures which were in the sea, and had life, died; and the third part of the ships were destroyed.

10 And the third angel sounded, and there fell a great star from heaven, burning as it were a lamp, and it fell upon the third part of the rivers, and upon the fountains of waters;

11 And the name of the star is called Wormwood: and the third

Revelation Chapters 8 & 9

part of the waters became wormwood; and many men died of the waters, because they were made bitter.

12 And the fourth angel sounded, and the third part of the sun was smitten, and the third part of the moon, and the third part of the stars; so as the third part of them was darkened, and the day shone not for a third part of it, and the night likewise.

13 And I beheld, and heard an angel flying through the midst of heaven, saying with a loud voice, Woe, woe, woe, to the inhabiters of the earth by reason of the other voices of the trumpet of the three angels, which are yet to sound!

Revelation 9

1 And the fifth angel sounded, and I saw a star fall from heaven unto the earth: and to him was given the key of the bottomless pit.

2 And he opened the bottomless pit; and there arose a smoke out of the pit, as the smoke of a great furnace; and the sun and the air were darkened by reason of the smoke of the pit.

3 And there came out of the smoke locusts upon the earth: and unto them was given power, as the scorpions of the earth have power.

4 And it was commanded them that they should not hurt the grass of the earth, neither any green thing, neither any tree; but only those men which have not the seal of God in their foreheads.

5 And to them it was given that they should not kill them, but that they should be tormented five months: and their torment was as the torment of a scorpion, when he striketh a man.

6 And in those days shall men seek death, and shall not find it; and shall desire to die, and death shall flee from them.

7 And the shapes of the locusts were like unto horses prepared unto battle; and on their heads were as it were crowns like gold, and their faces were as the faces of men.

8 And they had hair as the hair of women, and their teeth were

Revelation Chapters 8 & 9

as the teeth of lions.

9 And they had breastplates, as it were breastplates of iron; and the sound of their wings was as the sound of chariots of many horses running to battle.

10 And they had tails like unto scorpions, and there were stings in their tails: and their power was to hurt men five months.

11 And they had a king over them, which is the angel of the bottomless pit, whose name in the Hebrew tongue is Abaddon, but in the Greek tongue hath his name Apollyon.

12 One woe is past; and, behold, there come two woes more hereafter.

13 And the sixth angel sounded, and I heard a voice from the four horns of the golden altar which is before God,

14 Saying to the sixth angel which had the trumpet, Loose the four angels which are bound in the great river Euphrates.

15 And the four angels were loosed, which were prepared for an hour, and a day, and a month, and a year, for to slay the third part of men.

16 And the number of the army of the horsemen were two hundred thousand thousand: and I heard the number of them.

17 And thus I saw the horses in the vision, and them that sat on them, having breastplates of fire, and of jacinth, and brimstone: and the heads of the horses were as the heads of lions; and out of their mouths issued fire and smoke and brimstone.

18 By these three was the third part of men killed, by the fire, and by the smoke, and by the brimstone, which issued out of their mouths.

19 For their power is in their mouth, and in their tails: for their tails were like unto serpents, and had heads, and with them they do hurt.

20 And the rest of the men which were not killed by these plagues yet repented not of the works of their hands, that they should not worship devils, and idols of gold, and silver, and brass, and stone, and of wood: which neither can see, nor hear,

nor walk:

21 Neither repented they of their murders, nor of their sorceries, nor of their fornication, nor of their thefts. (Revelation chapter's 8 & 9)

Comparative Info on the "two witnesses"

Apostle John & associate	<u>The two olive trees & the two candlesticks.</u> Rev. 11:3, 4
Prophecy of Rev. chap. 10 & 11, is wedged in between 2nd woe and the 3rd woe.	Prophecy of Rev. chap. 10 & 11 is wedged in between the 2nd woe and the 3rd woe.
Prophetic events of Matthew 16:28; John 21:21, 22; and Rev. 10:11, begin at the end of the 2nd woe the and end at the beginning of the 3rd woe (Rev. 11:14).	Prophetic events of Revelation chapter eleven begin at the end of the "2nd woe" and end at beginning of the "3rd woe" (Revelation 11:14).
Apostle John & associate prophets of the LORD.	The 2 witnesses (2 prophets of the LORD. Rev. 11: 4, 3, 10), are personified.
"You must prophesy again" Rev. 10:11	The two witnesses "shall prophesy." Rev. 11:3
"disciples should not die." John 21:23	Cannot be killed by man. Revelation 11:5, 6

Comparative Info on the "two witnesses"

Shall prophesy between 2nd woe & 3rd woe. Rev. 10:11 Rev. 11:14, 15

Shall prophesy between 2nd woe & 3rd woe. Rev. 11:3 Rev. 11:14, 15

"Shall terry till I come" John 21:22

The two witnesses tarry till Christ comes in His kingdom. Rev. 11:14-17

"shall not taste of death, till they see the Son of man coming in His kingdom." Matt. 16:28

-"beast" kills the witnesses at the end of prophecy Rev 11:7
-After 3.5 days the 2 witnesses are resurrected. Rev. 11:11
-Taken to heaven. Rev. 11:12
-See Christ coming in His kingdom. Rev. 11:15-17

Is Apostle John Still Alive Today *By: Philip Mitanidis*..........199
Questions

QUESTIONS

1). How many apostles did Jesus have?
2). How many of these apostles were ordained by Him?
3). After Judas Iscariot hung himself, who replaced him?
4). How many apostles after Christ's resurrection were killed?
5). By Scripture, can you name the apostles that were killed?
6). How many apostles were told that they had to "prophesy again"?
7). How many apostles were told that they were not going to "taste of death" till Jesus comes in His kingdom?
8). How are these apostles able to live and work without drawing curious men and women to themselves and exposing their 2,000 year old longevity?
9). What is the purpose of keeping these apostles alive till Jesus comes?
10). The apostles, who are still alive today, are they eventually going to reveal themselves to us?
11). What do you expect these apostles to say or do, when they reveal themselves to us?
12). Where are these apostles going to be when they reveal themselves to us?
13). Will people like what they hear when the apostles begin their "testimony" and "prophecy"?
14). Why do the wicked, from around the world, want to kill

two apostles?

15). How were these apostles going to defend themselves from the attempts upon their lives?

16). After the apostles finish their testimony and prophesying, who manages to kill the apostles?

17). What are the wicked, throughout the world, going to do when they see the apostles dead?

18). What are the wicked going to do with their dead bodies?

19). How long will the dead bodies of the apostles going to remain in one of the streets of Jerusalem?

20). Eventually, what is going to happen to the apostles dead bodies?

21). What is the purpose of the apostle's mission?

22). Will the apostles accomplish their mission before they are killed?

23). Who and how many are going to die in Jerusalem after the apostles are killed?

24). Between what two events are chapters 10 & 11 of the book of Revelation wedged in?

25). How many devastating plagues are going to be unleashed by the seven angels upon the wicked and upon the earth?

26). What is going to be the outcome of the human race?

27). What is going to be the outcome of planet earth and its young sun when Christ comes the 2nd time to earth?

28). Who is or what is the "beast" from the bottomless pit?

29). What is the bottomless pit or what is the meaning of the bottomless pit?

30). Those individuals who crucified Jesus Christ, are they going to see Christ come the 2nd time to earth?

31). What is the "spirit of prophecy"?

32). What is the "testimony of Jesus"?

33). Who provided the "prophecy" that is in the book of Revelation; and who wrote it?

Questions

34). When Jesus Christ comes the 2nd time to earth, where is He going to take His penitent people?
35). Where was Apostle John exiled by the Roman senate for preaching Jesus Christ and His Gospel?
36). For how long was Apostle John exiled?
37). What did the apostles receive from Jesus Christ the LORD in the upper room?
38). After His resurrection, to whom did Jesus say, "touch Me not" and why?
39). What are the warnings to people who add or delete words to the book of Revelation?
40). What are the blessings to people who read the book of Revelation?
41). Why are the "two witnesses" wearing "sackcloth" clothing?
42). Is Apostle Peter still alive today?
43). To whom was Apostle Peter refereeing to when he said to Jesus Christ, "LORD, what shall this man do?"
44). Since Apostle john and his associate are kept alive for the past 2,000 years , by the word of Christ the LORD, what significance does the longevity of the apostles have for you?

48458401R00112

Made in the USA
Charleston, SC
03 November 2015